Argente Gerbil

U.K. Price
£5.50

A PETKEEPER'S GUIDE TO

HAMSTERS
& GERBILS

Young male Yellow Hamster

Variegated Rat

A PETKEEPER'S GUIDE TO

HAMSTERS
& GERBILS

**A superbly illustrated introduction to keeping
hamsters, gerbils, rats, mice and chinchillas**

David Alderton

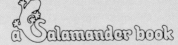

a Salamander book
Published by Salamander Books Limited
LONDON • NEW YORK

A Salamander Book

ISBN 0 86101 266 6

Distributed in the UK by Hodder and Stoughton Services,
P.O.Box 6, Mill Road, Dunton Green, Sevenoaks, Kent TN13 2XX.

Standard Chinchilla

Credits

Editor: Geoff Rogers   Designer: Graeme Campbell
Colour reproductions:
York House
Filmset: SX Composing Ltd.
Printed in Belgium by Henri Proost & Cie, Turnhout.

Author

David Alderton's abiding interest in the field of pet care and natural history began with the study of veterinary medicine at Cambridge University. Now the author of over 20 books, many with a particular emphasis on 'exotic' pets, David still finds time to contribute regularly to general and specialist periodicals in the UK and overseas. In addition to writing, David has always kept and bred a variety of animals and birds, and now runs a highly respected service that offers advice on the needs of animals kept in domestic and commercial environments. Through his consultancy work he has been closely involved in the development of safe non-toxic bedding material for small mammals and is fully conversant with current developments relating to their care.

Consultant

Chris Henwood has kept rodents since his school days and, although he has a wide interest in all forms of animal and plant life, his main interest still lies in this area. He has written several books and articles on the subject of rodents, their care and their genetics. He regularly appears on television and radio programmes as an expert on small animals and has advised a number of programme makers on aspects of rodents and their care. He is a National and International Judge of Hamsters and a founder member of both the Small Mammal Genetics Circle (SMGC) and the National Association of Private Animal Keepers (NAPAK). He maintains a wide collection of animals, including a number of rarely seen rodents and is believed to be one of the few non-zoological collections to have successfully bred the Rock Cavy.

Contents

Introduction

Keeping and breeding small rodents both as pets and for exhibition purposes is a relatively recent pastime, which dates back to the late 1800s. At that time, various forms of 'fancy' mouse began to emerge in domesticated stock. These early mutations were the forerunners of the many varieties seen today. Nevertheless, fancy mice had been known as pets in ancient Japan.

It was perhaps natural that, with the rise of the mouse fancy, fancy rats would also start to gain support. Initially, however, they did not achieve the popularity of their smaller relatives. Indeed, the history of fancy rats has been rather chequered in the past, but now they enjoy a considerable following.

Two new species of rodents – gerbils and hamsters – have become widely accepted as pets during the present century. Indeed, it now seems strange to regard both the popular Mongolian Gerbil and Golden Hamster as relative newcomers in the pet world.

A number of distinctive varieties are now recognized, and new forms are still being developed.

In contrast, chinchillas have a rather different history to the other subjects of this book, being kept originally for their distinctive fur. Yet they too are now being bred in an ever-increasing range of colour forms, and are becoming pets. Other rodents, notably the Russian Hamster, seem set to grow in popularity as pets as more people appreciate the charm of these mammals.

The creatures featured in this guide cannot be moved freely across many international frontiers, since in common with other pets, such as dogs, they can be carriers of rabies, the viral disease that is invariably fatal for humans. They must undergo a period of quarantine therefore, on entering the country. Check on this point with the relevant authority – usually the agricultural department – before you plan to move any stock from one country to another.

Introducing the rodents

In spite of a noticeable variation in their size, shape and overall appearance, all the pets covered in this book are related. They belong to the order Rodentia, and are commonly known as rodents. This group accounts for no less than 40 percent of all mammalian species, and 1,702 rodents have been identified so far.

In Part Two of the book we consider the biology, care, breeding and colour forms of gerbils, hamsters, mice, rats and chinchillas in detail. Here, we review some important features of rodents in general and reflect on their suitability as pets.

General features
Rodents are highly adaptable creatures with a worldwide distribution; there are species living in every possible terrain, from deserts to frozen tundra. Perhaps not surprisingly, rodents are relatively tolerant of temperature changes. Studies involving the popular Mongolian Gerbil, for example, have shown that these creatures will tolerate temperatures from about -18°C(0°F) to over 38°C(100°F). In most cases, however, the optimum appears to be about 20°C(68°F). Rodents which originate in arid areas are used to a dry environment. Gerbils, for example, are affected by relative humidity readings in excess of 50 percent. Although this does not appear to harm them, their fur becomes fluffed up and matted.

A feature common to all rodents is their ability to gnaw, and indeed, their name is derived from *rodere,* which is the Latin verb 'to gnaw'. This habit, which has made rodents such severe pests of crops and foodstuffs throughout the world, stems from the unusual arrangement of their teeth. The sharp incisor teeth at the front of the mouth are responsible for their immense capacity for destruction.

Popular pet rodents

The rodents featured in the book are shown here approximately in scale to one another. The chinchilla is more closely related to guinea pigs than to the other rodents shown.

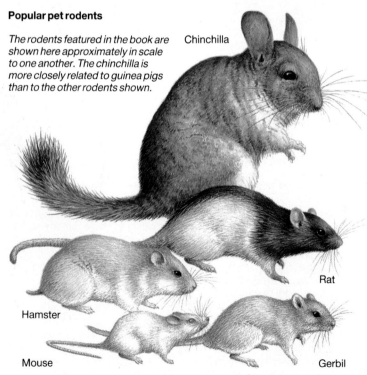

Chinchilla

Rat

Hamster

Mouse

Gerbil

Hamster skull and teeth

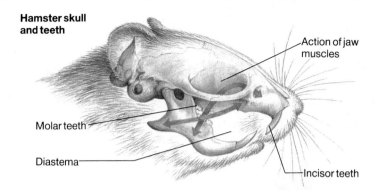

Action of jaw muscles

Molar teeth

Diastema

Incisor teeth

Above: *The teeth and jaw action are very significant for rodents. Any malformation of the incisors at the front of the mouth is serious.*

The molar teeth at the back of the mouth, or the pre-molars if these are present, grind the food into smaller pieces for swallowing. Pre-molars have been lost completely in the suborder Myomorpha, which includes rats, mice, hamsters and gerbils. (See illustration above.)

Between the molars and the incisors there is a gap, known as the diastema, where there are no teeth. This gap allows the cheeks to be closed in behind the incisors, enabling these rodents to continue gnawing while only selective particles are being swallowed.

Since the incisors are in constant and heavy use, they gradually become worn down. To compensate, they continue growing throughout the animal's life. It is vital, therefore, that the upper and lower incisor teeth actually meet at the front of the mouth. Any deviation from this pattern will spell disaster since, ultimately, the animal will no longer be able to eat, and the distorted teeth will strike the opposite jaw. For this reason, always check the mouth of a rodent before buying it. It is possible to cut the teeth back if necessary, but there is evidence to suggest that the problem is inherited. Therefore, do not use animals with this trait for breeding purposes.

Three families, notably the hamsters, have evolved a novel and extremely effective means of storing food. These animals use cheek pouches, which are extensive structures extending all the way back from the mouth to the shoulder. In hamsters, the pouches are simply an expansion of the cheeks, with the same mucous membrane lining as occurs inside the mouth. Rodents can empty these pouches as necessary, although blockages do occasionally occur, which need to be remedied promptly. It is surprising how much food small mammals can tuck into these pouches. The Common Hamster (*Cricetus cricetus*) has been known to store as much as 90kg (198lb) of food in this way during its life.

Above: *A pet gerbil investigates the world from the snug security of its owner's clothing. Once tame, most rodents make very amenable pets.*

13

In common with other herbivores, such as sheep, rodents feeding on plants are themselves incapable of digesting the carbohydrate present in the form of cellulose. Although they lack the elaborate stomach of many herbivores, rodents still rely on a beneficial group of bacteria to undertake this task. These bacteria possess the enzymes, known as cellulases, that break down the cellulose. They are located in the caecal sacs of the large intestine, corresponding to the human appendix. But because they work in the lower part of the gut, the rodents cannot benefit directly, since absorption of food materials takes place in the small intestine further forward in the digestive system. In order to overcome this problem, rodents actually re-ingest the partially digested food when it has been voided from the anus. These motions are relatively loose and contain not only partly digested food but also vitamins synthesized by the bacteria. They are quite unlike the dry faecal pellets typically associated with rodents.

As a pet owner, it is important to realize that consumption of faecal matter – a practice known as coprophagy – is essential to your animal's well-being. Clearly, a cage with a wire mesh floor tends to prevent the consumption of such faecal matter as the animals' droppings will fall out of reach. (See page 106 for chinchilla cages.) Over-zealous cleaning can also cause similar problems.

Rodents as pets
It is partly rodents' adaptibility that has led to their popularity as pets. They are not difficult to keep, and they tend to breed freely, which has given rise to a wide range of colour forms. This has led to selective breeding, also known as 'fancying', with the resulting progeny often being shown competitively. Rodents, in spite of their sharp incisors, are generally docile, especially once they are used to being handled. Their low cost and modest needs in terms of

Below: *Showing small mammals is a popular pastime worldwide. Here, a judge examines a hamster at a show. He is checking the colour, condition and appearance (type).*

Above: *Rodents, such as this hamster, are ideal children's pets, although relatively shortlived. Adult supervision is recommended, yet most rodents will not bite readily.*

accommodation and food have led them to become widely popular as children's pets in many regions of the world.

The only drawback in this respect is that most species, even after being bred in captivity for countless generations, tend to be nocturnal, becoming more active after dark when children are likely to be in bed. This trait is reflected by the relatively large eyes of mice, for example. In some instances, this nocturnal habit is a safeguard against predators. In gerbils, however, it ensures that the animals are not exposed to the harsh rays of the sun in the desert environment in which they live. To avoid losing too much fluid by evaporation, gerbils, like many other rodents, live in cool sheltered burrows below ground during the daytime. (See also page 42.)

Although rodents, especially rats and mice, have proved to be carriers of severe, if not fatal, illnesses for

humans, this need not be a serious worry if you are thinking of keeping the fancy forms now available. These have been bred in captivity for very many generations, and are maintained in sanitary conditions. Indeed, they are widely used for research purposes, where healthy stock is of paramount importance in obtaining meaningful results from such work.

While the use of rodents (and other animals) in research is often criticized, it is undeniable that this has provided great insight into the biology of these creatures. A vast amount of information relating to their nutritional requirements, breeding stimuli and disease susceptibilities has been amassed in laboratories throughout the world. Most pet rodents are in fact descendants of stock bred in laboratories. The same qualities which attracted scientists, such as a rat's intelligence, have proved to be just as appealing to pet owners. Indeed, it is doubtful if either gerbils or hamsters would have become widely kept as pets if it were not for their initial value to researchers.

Sexing rodents

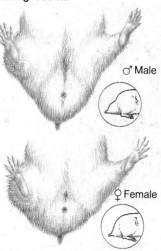

Above: *Sexing most rodents is fairly easy. The distinction is based on the ano-genital distance; this is longer in the male, as shown in the hamster.*

15

Accommodation and equipment

The housing you provide must reflect the rodent's natural habits as far as possible. The type of accommodation required will vary, therefore, according to the species concerned. Gerbils, for example, must be able to burrow into the floor covering of their enclosure.

DIY housing

Probably the simplest means of housing smaller rodents is to use a fish tank. Plastic ones are preferable, because glass aquariums now almost always have a silicone sealant on the inner surfaces. Rodents can gnaw this away and will escape if one of the panes of glass becomes loose. The urine of mice and rats especially may soil the sealant, and this can prove difficult to clean. Glass aquariums are also significantly heavier and more fragile than their plastic counterparts. Moulded acrylic tanks are ideal, since there

are no loose edges for the rodents to gnaw and they can be washed out thoroughly and easily whenever necessary.

The depth of the container is important; it must be deep enough to ensure that the rodents cannot escape. Certainly, if several of both sexes do get free and move to an inaccessible place, such as beneath the floorboards, you are likely to encounter serious problems. Their quarters must therefore be as secure as possible. Although they will not be able to climb directly up the sides of a fish tank, they could use a box in their quarters to reach the top. The depth of the container is particularly significant for burrowing gerbils, since a thick layer of bedding is required. For this reason, it is best to choose a plastic aquarium about 45cm (18in) deep, therefore, rather than opting for one only 30cm (12in) deep.

Ideally, fit a secure lid to ensure

Plastic aquarium for housing gerbils

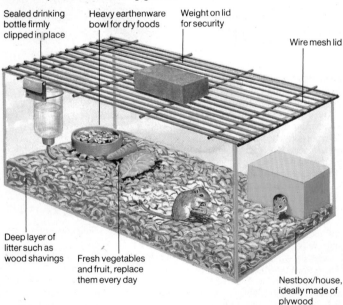

Sealed drinking bottle firmly clipped in place

Heavy earthenware bowl for dry foods

Weight on lid for security

Wire mesh lid

Deep layer of litter such as wood shavings

Fresh vegetables and fruit, replace them every day

Nestbox/house, ideally made of plywood

Above: *A one-piece plastic fish tank provides the ideal accommodation for small rodents, such as gerbils. The plastic will get scratched in time* but it will not absorb urine smells and is easy to clean. Choose one about 45cm (18in) deep for added security and equip it as shown here.

that the rodents do not climb out. Metal vivarium lids, manufactured to cover the quarters of reptiles and amphibians, are useful for this purpose. They are supplied with ventilation panels and an inspection hatch. Most designs also incorporate an aperture to take a light fitting, which will not be required in this instance. As an added security measure, therefore, place a weight on top so that the hole is covered and the lid cannot be dislodged. This is especially important if you have a cat because, apart from the risk of the rodents escaping, there is also a possibility that your cat may attempt to disturb the lid and catch them.

For many years, rodent fanciers had to keep their charges in wooden-panelled cages with a wire mesh roof or front. This is probably the least satisfactory accommodation for rodents. While a clear plastic fish tank may become scratched, and its appearance will deteriorate over a period of time, it does permit good visibility from all sides. It also has the advantage that it will not absorb the lingering odours of urine, which are most noticeable with rats and mice. This is not the case with wood, and furthermore, rodents can easily chew through a softwood cage. Stout plywood may be more successful but you will need to be alert if signs of gnawing appear. Since young mice can escape through even 1.25cm (0.5in) square mesh, the sides are best solid with mesh forming the roof. This will also prevent debris being scattered over the floor of the room.

A wooden framework covered with wire mesh may prove the most suitable method of housing a chinchilla. This will help to prevent its delicate coat from becoming soiled. Alternatively, use a cage constructed entirely of wire mesh. Although this is suitable for keeping chinchillas in a shed or similar outbuilding, it is not a particularly attractive option in the home. Chinchillas, by virtue of their size, need more space than the other rodents featured in this book.

Manufactured cages

The more traditional type of rodent cages available in a pet store are constructed from sheet metal. There are various designs. Before buying a cage, look carefully for any signs of rough edges that could injure your pet quite seriously. Also consider ease of access and the strength of the door fastening. Clearly, you will need to be able to

Above: *This plastic housing system for small rodents is attractive and easy to extend. Take care with older hamsters; they may become too fat to move through the tubes.*

clean the cage out thoroughly with minimum disturbance. A sliding tray may be useful, but ensure that sunflower or other large seeds will not block its movement. Do not be surprised if a plastic tray gets gnawed.

The size of cage you need will depend to some extent on the number of rodents you wish to keep together, but generally always choose as large a cage as possible. More detailed information on housing for various types of small mammals can be found under the individual sections in Part Two. The more expensive cages tend to be the most suitable and are perhaps less likely to rust prematurely.

The spacing of the bars is important for your pet's welfare. It should be less than 1.25cm (0.5in), otherwise the rodents may rub their snouts between the bars, causing hair loss and possible injury. In an emergency, however, a bird cage can be used to provide separate accommodation if no other suitable housing is available.

As there will be times when you will need to wash and clean the rodents' quarters completely, cages with a heavy duty plastic base and a detachable wire top, similar in many ways to modern bird cages, have become increasingly popular. Accommodation of this type is used for laboratory rodents, where ease of maintenance is viewed as a vital design consideration. Laboratory cages can also be used to house domestic pets, but the majority of suppliers are not keen to sell individual units to members of the general public.

The most recent development in rodent housing is an ingenious interconnecting plastic tubular system suitable for the smaller species. It is available in a range of colours and the units can be joined together to create housing of various shapes and sizes. Although eye-catching and versatile, this system is not without its disadvantages. While young rodents can move through the tubes without difficulty, older, more obese animals may encounter problems, and could even get stuck. These units are relatively costly, and you will probably need to buy a second unit, as the basic kit usually provides only a small area. Cleaning, too, can prove troublesome. On the whole, however, these units do offer an attractive, inventive, yet natural setting for burrowing rodents.

Transportation and showing
When buying rodents, it is best to take a small wooden box with ventilation holes and a sliding door that can be firmly closed. Pet stores tend only to have cardboard boxes available, and these, with their gaps for ventilation, are no match for a rodent's teeth, which can create

considerable damage within minutes. Apart from the inconvenience that may result, especially on a long journey, your newly acquired pet or breeding stock could even be lost before you arrive home. Remember, also, that rodents will succumb to heatstroke, and so take care not to leave them confined in boxes in cars on warm sunny days.

Exhibition rodents are normlly transported to shows in boxes, before being transferred to the show cage itself. The internationally known Maxey show cage for mice, named after Walter Maxey – popularly regarded today as the 'Father of the Mouse Fancy' – differs somewhat from conventional housing. It is designed for ease of movement, straightforward cleaning and rapid access, which facilitates judging, since the animals are removed from their cages to be examined by the judge. Similar cages are used for exhibition stock of other species.

Keep show cages clean and ensure that your rodents feel at home in them. Judges award points on the basis of features such as colour, type and condition of the animal, and deductions may be

Below: *If you decide to show your hamsters, they must be exhibited, or benched, in the correct type of cage, described as a pen. This is constructed to a standard design and painted as shown here. Use only sawdust as a floor covering.*

Typical hamster cage

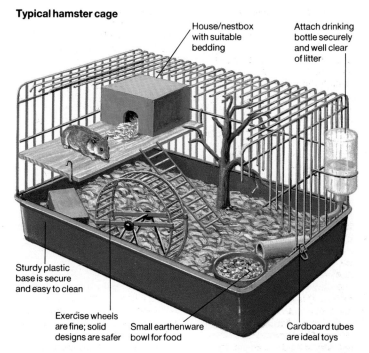

House/nestbox with suitable bedding

Attach drinking bottle securely and well clear of litter

Sturdy plastic base is secure and easy to clean

Exercise wheels are fine; solid designs are safer

Small earthenware bowl for food

Cardboard tubes are ideal toys

Above: *This form of cage is very popular for housing hamsters, yet it can also be used for other small rodents, such as gerbils. Remember to remove the wheel if the cage is used for gerbils, however. Check that all fitments, such as any branches, are held firmly in position and cannot be dislodged, otherwise they could cause serious injury.*

made if the cage is dirty, or the animal concerned is nervous and resents being handled.

Equipping the cage
Here, we consider the best choice of bedding materials for keeping rodents and review the food containers and toys suitable for equipping the cage or quarters.

Bedding Similar bedding is required for all rodents. First, you will need an absorbent floor covering. Sawdust is traditionally used for this purpose, but ensure that it does not contain toxic chemicals. Rodents may eat their bedding, and losses have been traced to contaminated sawdust and wood-shavings. Different types of sawdust are available, with softwood sawdust proving the most absorbent. Pine sawdust is useful for this reason and tends to be white

in colour. Darker coloured sawdust is likely to have originated from hardwoods, and is invariably much finer, which reduces its absorptive capacity. Hardwood sawdust is also more likely to irritate the eyes and nose if used as bedding.

Wood-shavings are coarser than sawdust and often cheaper, but you will need a thicker layer to cover the same area effectively. A further consideration is that while shavings will not adhere as readily to fresh food as sawdust will, and are thus less likely to be consumed as a result, they do tend to conceal stale food. Most pet stores sell packets of sawdust and wood-shavings. You may need to buy a relatively large quantity, but neither is expensive.

Wood-wool, frequently used in the packing of fragile goods and fruit, is not recommended as a bedding material. These very thin

19

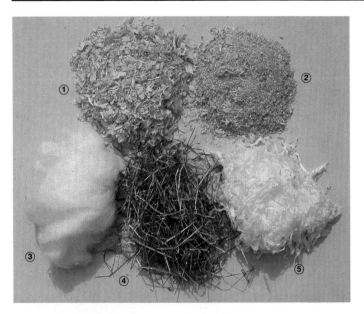

Above: Several materials are suitable for use as litter and bedding. **1** *Wood shavings. These are ideal as a basic lining material; they are fairly absorbent, easy to use and safe for the animals.* **2** *Sawdust. Use the softer white sawdust from pine and other* softwoods rather than the darker, harder types.* **3** *Natural fibre. These safe natural fibre bedding materials are suitable for smaller animals.* **4** *Meadow hay. Use good quality, clean hay free from mould spores.* **5** *Paper bedding. This is the shredded type suitable for a bed.*

strips of wood still possess rigidity, and could become embedded around the neck or a limb, with serious consequences. Damp peat is also occasionally used as a floor covering for rodent cages, but unfortunately it becomes very dusty as it dries out. Nor is sand really suitable, by virtue of its abrasive nature and poor absorptive capacity.

It is best to use only materials which are marketed especially for use as small-animal bedding, since other types of material that might seem ideal, such as cotton wool, can prove fatal if swallowed. Nylon of any kind may become twisted around the legs, causing injury; while wool, if ingested, is likely to cause a blockage in the digestive system of the animal.

Hay can be used, but check that it is fresh and free from moulds. Fungal spores will almost certainly be present in the hay, however, and if the bedding is likely to become damp this moisture will encourage the development of moulds.

A recent innovation in the field of small-animal care is granulated paper bedding. This paper, the same type as is used in the manufacture of tea bags, is highly absorbent and safe, being essentially free from dust, unlike either sawdust or wood-shavings. A coarser grade, sold as shredded paper, is ideal for providing a sleeping and nesting area within the cage. You can also use paper towelling cut into strips instead.

Many manufactured cages incorporate a secluded sleeping area where bedding can be placed. If you are using a fish tank, you can either place the bedding loose in a corner or, better still, use it to line a plywood box placed within the accommodation. Again, bearing in mind the gnawing propensity of rodents, use small nails to assemble the pieces of such a box rather than glue, which could prove toxic.

Food and water pots Food pots need to be suitably robust. Although stainless steel pots can be used, these are easily tipped over by rodents. Glazed earthenware pots are better, being heavier yet equally easy to clean. Both seeds and fresh food can be offered in such pots. There is no need to use one of the larger sizes; indeed these will occupy an excessively large area in the cage and may prevent your pet moving around freely.

The easiest and most secure method of providing water is by means of a sealed water bottle with a spout, operating on the gravity flow system. The position of the bottle is important. Check that it is within easy reach of the rodents, but that it does not touch the bedding. If this happens, it is likely that capillary action will draw water from the bottle and saturate the bedding.

Make sure that the water bottle fits firmly in place, and that it cannot be accidentally dislodged by the rodents' chewing. It will not be difficult to fit a water bottle in a commercially produced cage, but may prove more difficult in a converted aquarium. It may be necessary to hang the bottle on a loop of wire into a corner of the enclosure. To do this, you may need to fit a purpose-built mesh roof, using a wooden framework positioned out of the rodents' reach.

Toys Hamsters in particular will frequently take advantage of a toy treadwheel in their quarters. Although this provides valuable exercise, treadwheels can develop into an addictive habit for the animal. If this appears to be happening, remove the wheel for periods. Avoid any designs in which the creature could get its foot stuck by accident. Those which are solid, even if made of plastic, are the safest option for this reason.

Pet rodents will also appreciate other simple toys. It is important for these animals to keep their incisor teeth in trim and giving them a small piece of wood cut from a tree will help in this regard. Since many rodents enjoy gnawing and stripping the bark off wood, this is a way of providing an inexpensive yet highly worthwhile plaything for your pet. You can also buy compressed seed toys, in shapes such as bells, for your pet to gnaw. These are not as useful as pieces of wood, however, especially for more wasteful eaters such as hamsters. Needless to say, plastic toys are not suitable for rodents; they will soon suffer from the attentions of those sharp incisor teeth and eventually be destroyed.

Always consider the size of toys in relation to the size of the rodents. For example, exercise wheels designed primarily for mice may not be suitable for hamsters. Cardboard tubes, such as those inside paper kitchen towel rolls, will certainly be too small for most rats, yet are appreciated by mice. You can dispose of them when they become chewed or soiled, although at first your pet may be reluctant to accept a replacement, and will sniff cautiously at the new item.

Outdoor accommodation

In some instances it may be necessary to keep your rodents in a shed or similar outbuilding. Indeed, most serious breeders of exhibition stock convert a shed specifically for the purpose.

Be sure to position the cage or cages correctly in relation to any windows in a shed. During hot weather the interior is likely to warm up rapidly, and this can kill rodents kept close to the window and in the direct rays of the sun. (This also applies in the home, of course, where a location in the corner of the room is best.) Curtains may be useful in a shed, and ideally you should be able to remove the windows, or at least open them, to provide adequate ventilation.

Take care to exclude cats, which even if they cannot reach the rodents may cause fatalities by harassing them over a period of time. To keep them out, fit wire mesh on the inside of the window and make a false door of wire mesh so that you can leave both the windows and door open on hot days without fear of stock losses. The wire mesh, if it is of suitable dimensions, will also help to stop the accidental escape of rodents from the shed.

Build shelving or a racking system to hold the cages, with a food store incorporated underneath. Metal dustbins are ideal for this purpose, since they will not attract rodents to the seed store, which can happen if food is left in paper sacks. Sacks may also get damp, spoiling their contents as a result. Also provide a dustbin for rubbish.

A work surface at a convenient height is useful, either for handling rodents out of their cage or simply for writing up breeding notes on stock. This need only be a piece of melamine-faced chipboard held up by brackets. A restraining frame is also handy. This is merely a four-sided frame with wooden sides of appropriate height which will enable you to assess the rodent on the work surface, without fear of it escaping or falling off. Such a frame is also useful when you are cleaning out the cage.

Clearly, there will be advantages in having a supply of electricity in the shed. During the winter, this will enable you to inspect the animals in the evening if necessary, and provide heating during severe weather. Electric tubular heaters with a thermostatic control, such as those used in greenhouses, are the safest option. It will pay dividends in terms of heating costs if you insulate the shed walls and roof with hardboard or similar material. If you are using artificial light to extend the period of daylight, incorporate suitable time-switches into the circuitry. Although not available from most pet stores, you should be able to obtain equipment of this type from specialist suppliers.

Right: *If your interest in keeping rodents becomes a passion, you may need to convert your shed.*

Garden shed converted to house rodents

A converted garden shed is ideal for housing small rodents. It provides considerable space for storage of foodstuffs, stock cages and show pens. A wallchart can be used with cage numbers to record breeding details and other information.

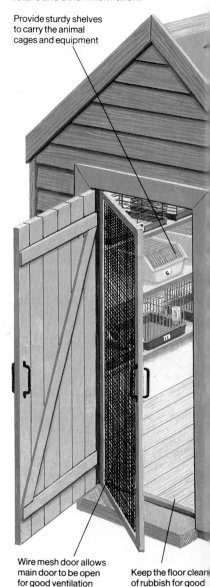

Provide sturdy shelves to carry the animal cages and equipment

Wire mesh door allows main door to be open for good ventilation

Keep the floor clean of rubbish for good

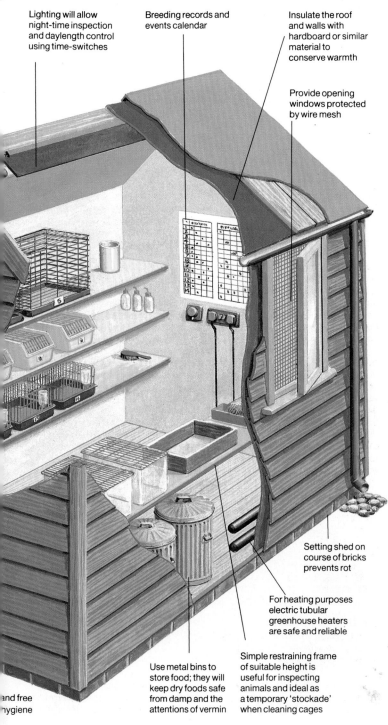

Lighting will allow night-time inspection and daylength control using time-switches

Breeding records and events calendar

Insulate the roof and walls with hardboard or similar material to conserve warmth

Provide opening windows protected by wire mesh

Setting shed on course of bricks prevents rot

For heating purposes electric tubular greenhouse heaters are safe and reliable

Use metal bins to store food; they will keep dry foods safe from damp and the attentions of vermin

Simple restraining frame of suitable height is useful for inspecting animals and ideal as a temporary 'stockade' when cleaning cages

and free hygiene

Feeding

Rodents are easy to feed. Most species will eat a wide range of seeds and fresh foods, including greenstuff and fruit. The use of rodents in laboratories has given us a clear picture of their nutritional needs and has in turn provided the financial stimulus for the production of pelleted diets for each species. These pellets contain all the known dietary requirements, but it is generally a good idea to supplement them with other foods. However, as laboratory feeds are not widely available to the petkeeper, it may be necessary to use rabbit pellets mixed with a variety of seeds and nuts as a substitute.

Seeds

Seeds can be divided into two groups on the basis of their nutritional value. The first group consists of the cereal seeds, such as oats, maize, wheat and barley, which are essentially energy foods, containing relatively high levels of carbohydrates compared with fats.

Whole oats have a rather sharp outer husk which can irritate the cheek pouches of hamsters in particular. This is less of a problem with crushed oats or with groats, which are whole, dehusked oats.

Maize (or 'corn') is available in several forms, of which flaked is probably the most useful. It is also available in a broken, or kibbled, form. The whole seed is very hard and rather large for smaller rodents. Both wheat and barley may be added to some seed mixtures.

Sunflower seeds and peanuts (groundnuts) make up the second group. These are popular with rodents, but contain significantly higher levels of fat than the cereals. Use them in moderation, therefore, to prevent obesity.

While it is possible to purchase ready-mixed food for rodents, you can mix together the individual ingredients yourself. To do this, combine roughly equal parts of oats, wheat, maize and rabbit pellets, with just a token amount of sunflower seeds and peanuts.

Keep all seeds dry, and avoid using any that appear dirty or that are mixed with a lot of debris, such as stones. Mouldy peanuts are especially dangerous, being the source of potent poisons known as aflatoxins. If the seed is old it may show signs of mites, which could cause your pet skin irritation.

Other foods

In addition to a basic seed ration, feeding your pet with various other foodstuffs will be beneficial. Wholemeal bread dried out in an oven and offered dry, is an excellent source of carbohydrate energy and, being hard, will also help to keep rodent's teeth in trim. Dog biscuits are also useful, especially if they are supplemented with vitamins and

Hamster feeding

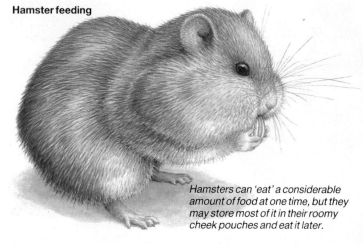

Hamsters can 'eat' a considerable amount of food at one time, but they may store most of it in their roomy cheek pouches and eat it later.

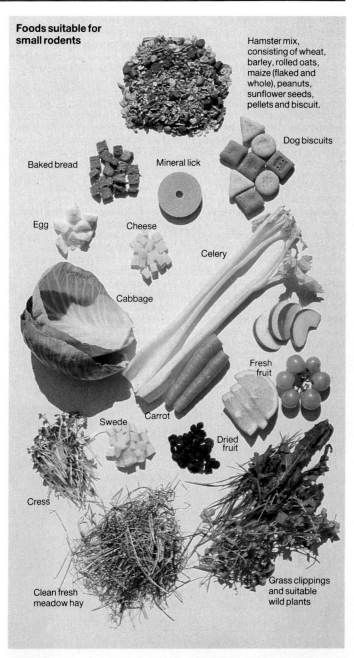

Foods suitable for small rodents

Hamster mix, consisting of wheat, barley, rolled oats, maize (flaked and whole), peanuts, sunflower seeds, pellets and biscuit.

Dog biscuits

Baked bread

Mineral lick

Egg

Cheese

Celery

Cabbage

Fresh fruit

Swede

Carrot

Dried fruit

Cress

Clean fresh meadow hay

Grass clippings and suitable wild plants

Above: *The above selection of food is suitable for hamsters and similar small mammals. Some of the items should be offered only as occasional treats. When feeding fresh fruit and vegetables, be sure to wash them thoroughly. Apart from the risk of pesticide residues, diseases can be transmitted by way of contaminated foods.*

25

minerals, which are likely to be deficient in a diet made up mostly of seeds. Alternatively, in some countries, special vitamin and mineral chews are produced for rodents. Similar products are also widely available in powder form. If you do use the powder, remember that it is best to sprinkle the required quantity over damp greenstuff, as it will not adhere readily to dry seed.

Your pets will appreciate a wide range of fruit and vegetables. Always wash fresh food. Apart from the risk of pesticide residues, diseases may occasionally be transmitted from contaminated fruit and greenstuff.

There is little nutritional value in lettuce, however, and other alternatives such as cress are preferable. You can give your pets cabbage occasionally, especially the coarser outer leaves, which are the most valuable in nutritional terms, and the coarse stems, which

are a challenge for their teeth. However, as with all such foods, offer only a restricted amount, since regular usage of brassicas (cabbage family) could have a depressant effect on the thyroid gland.

If your pet rodent is not used to greenfood, start with only a little at first, otherwise diarrhoea is almost certain to result. Among wild plants that can be given in moderation are dandelions (*Taraxacum officinale*) and chickweed (*Stellaria media*). Some plants, such as buttercups (*Ranunculus* sp.) and ragwort (*Senecio* sp.), are poisonous though, so only feed those which are known to be safe. Root vegetables such as carrots are also valuable as food items, being available throughout the year when greenstuff may be in short supply.

Always remove perishable food from the cage before it shrivels or becomes mouldy. This is particularly important with bread and milk, which is sometimes provided for breeding rodents to satisfy the higher level of protein they need in their diet. It is not essential, however, and is very messy if the food pot is knocked

Below: A Golden Hamster feeding on sunflower seeds. Since these contain a relatively high level of oil (fat), use them sparingly in a mixture to avoid causing obesity.

over. Clean up any such spillage before it can turn mouldy. If you make up a softfood of any kind for your pet, ensure that it is moist, but not awash with fluid.

Hard-boiled egg, cut into small pieces, is another fresh food you can give occasionally. Pieces of cheese can also be offered as titbits.

More specific details about feeding are given in the individual sections in Part Two. It is worth noting here, however, that chinchillas are fed essentially on special pellets rather than a mixed diet. These may not be available from all pet stores, so it is worth enquiring about a source of supply when obtaining a chinchilla. Other foods can be obtained without difficulty in most instances, but groats may not be as easy to find as the other seeds. All these items can be purchased from seed merchants and specialist suppliers.

Water
Always ensure that a fresh supply of water is available to all rodents, even though some species appear not to need it. This applies especially to animals living on a

Above: A Standard Chinchilla enjoys a piece of apple. Be sure to provide rodents with a varied diet of both fresh and dried foods, plus a readily available supply of water.

dried diet. Fresh food such as greenstuff contains very high levels of water, which rodents are able to utilize, so that they are likely to drink less fluid.

You can also administer water-soluble vitamin and mineral preparations via drinking water, but this is probably less satisfactory than using a powder sprinkled over food, since most rodents will drink relatively little fluid.

Clean out the drinking bottle daily when such tonics are used, and, in any event, change the water every day. Special bottle brushes are ideal for keeping the glass or plastic container free from any trace of algal growth, which is otherwise likely to build up over a period of time. Also make sure the spout is kept clean. If you use any detergent or disinfectant during the cleaning process, remember to rinse both the bottle and the spout very thoroughly before refilling the container.

Health care

Rodents, in spite of their relatively short lives, are nevertheless quite healthy creatures. Here, we consider how to cope with minor injuries, and review a selection of the bacterial, viral, parasitic and inherited conditions that may afflict rodents in captivity.

It is difficult to give tablets to rodents and injections are obviously stressful, especially as they almost always need to be repeated. Therefore, medication is most easily given via the drinking water. Particular care must be taken, however, with antibiotics, as rodents depend upon the bacteria in their gut for the digestion of cellulose. Since antibiotics do not discriminate between harmful and beneficial bacteria, they can be hazardous. Indeed, many antibiotics can prove toxic for rodents, including the most commonly used types such as penicillin, tylosin, erythromycin and lincomycin. Always seek veterinary advice, therefore, even in countries where antibiotics can be freely purchased.

Injuries from fighting
Avoid overcrowding at all costs, since this can lead to serious outbreaks of fighting. Whereas gerbils tend to be social animals, hamsters are solitary by nature and are best kept on their own for much of their lives; they often fight savagely if kept in groups for any length of time. Rodents' sharp teeth are formidable weapons in a fight and are capable of inflicting serious, if not fatal, damage to an opponent. Keep a close watch for signs of aggression and separate potential combatants before serious injury occurs. This applies especially to hamsters during the mating period.

If there is any bleeding and a large area of skin appears damaged, take your pet to a veterinarian for advice. Dab minor injuries several times with an antiseptic lotion; they should then heal satisfactorily. In some cases, however, especially if the wound is deep, infection may develop, leading to the formation of an abscess that will require rapid veterinary treatment. It is possible

for rodents to recover successfully from abscesses, but you must consider whether the cost of treatment, especially for an older individual, is worthwhile.

Chinchillas' wounds may well turn septic, since these animals are particularly susceptible to infection by *Pseudomonas* bacteria, which will thrive in deep wounds such as those inflicted by a bite.

Breathing difficulties
Rodents as a group are prone to respiratory problems. Do not be too worried, however, if your rodent sneezes several times in succession. This does not necessarily indicate an illness, but may simply be irritation caused by the dust from its bedding.

Various respiratory diseases are recognized, of which murine respiratory mycoplasmosis, affecting rats and mice, is a relatively common example. This is known as a mixed infection since, in addition to mycoplasmas (which share characteristics with both bacteria and viruses), other bacteria and viruses are often involved. Apart from snuffling, other more serious signs may be associated with this disease, especially in rats. The disease can spread from the respiratory system to the middle ear, which in turn gives rise to neurological signs. Affected animals may then suffer a loss of coordination and start circling. Successful treatment is difficult at this stage.

In many cases, however, an infection may not be very apparent. Environmental factors will affect the development of clinical signs of the disease. For example, dirty surroundings create a build-up of ammonia which in turn damages a rodent's respiratory tract, making it more susceptible to this kind of infection. Overcrowding also favours spread of the disease, as mycoplasmas tend to be passed directly from rodent to rodent. It is important, therefore, to separate affected stock, and give these animals a safe antibiotic effective against mycoplasmas. Repeated

Above: *Rodents can inflict serious injuries on each other if they fight. This male Russian Hamster was attacked by its potential mate.*

treatment may be necessary to clear the infection, especially if more than one rodent is affected.

Digestive problems

These range from simple cases of diarrhoea to serious infections that can cause permanent damage.

Diarrhoea, often described as 'scour' in the case of rodents, is not a disease itself but a symptom that can result from a number of causes. These need not all be infectious. Indeed, feeding excessive amounts of greenfood will almost certainly precipitate scouring in rodents, but it is usually self-limiting in this case and not fatal.

Tyzzer's Disease, which is a bacterial infection caused by *Bacillus piliformis*, can lead to high mortality, particularly in young rodents. Diarrhoea is frequently seen in the course of this disease. Affected rodents show characteristic signs of ill-health, adopting a hunched posture and being reluctant to move. Their fur is held away from the body and looks in poor condition. This infection is more likely to be encountered in a breeding group, rather than in an animal kept on its own. If Tyzzer's Disease is suspected, diagnosis can only be confirmed accurately by a post-mortem examination, notably of the liver, where the presence of

the bacteria can usually be detected.

There are various other bacteria which may occasionally give rise to similar symptoms. It may be possible to treat some animals successfully with antibiotics if medication is given early during the course of the disease. Take particular care when purchasing stock, since symptoms may develop shortly afterwards. Never introduce newcomers to an established colony before quarantining them in separate accommodation for a fortnight or so. Hopefully, this will minimize the risk of disease being introduced to an established colony.

It is interesting to note that gerbils tend to be resistant to most infectious diseases, although they will succumb to Tyzzer's Disease.

'Wet tail' is a highly infectious disease found in hamsters, again affecting the digestive tract. Known more technically as 'proliferative ileitis' or 'regional ileitis', this disease can reach epidemic proportions. It affects the lower part of the small intestine known as the ileum, which becomes inflamed and thickened, restricting the passage of food through the gut. The description 'wet tail' stems from the scouring that dampens the fur around the hamster's tail region. Loss of appetite, followed by wasting, then become apparent and death occurs between two and seven days after the initial signs.

The actual cause remains something of a mystery. It appears that the disease may result in part from infection by a bacterium known as *Escherichia coli*, but other bacteria may be involved in the characteristic changes of the ileum. Treatment is difficult and not generally successful, partly because the scouring removes vital body fluids that are difficult to replace. Using antibiotics is often counterproductive since they destroy beneficial bacteria in the intestine. Thorough disinfection after an outbreak is essential.

Newly weaned hamsters up to eight weeks old are considered to be the most susceptible to this disease. Because the stress of weaning may precipitate an attack, keep litters separately rather than mix them, which simply imposes additional stress. It seems likely that the infection may be contracted from the female before weaning. As there may also be a genetic resistance to infection, it is best not to use affected animals for breeding purposes, even if they recover from the disease.

'Diarrhoea of Infant Mice', caused by a virus, can result in high losses of young mice. Unfortunately, this infection is liable to impair the intestinal function permanently, even if the mouse does recover. Judicious use of antibiotics may save sick animals by reducing the risk of secondary bacterial infection, but it is not always recommended because of the lasting damage caused by this disease.

Viral diseases
A large number of viral infections are known in rodents, but the vast majority are unlikely to be encountered by the pet owner. At least twenty have been identified in rats and mice alone, and in some cases, they can be infected without showing any apparent clinical signs of illness. These have been identified in the course of using this group of animals for research purposes. Unfortunately, it is not possible to combat viral diseases with antibiotics.

Mouse Pox is probably the most serious viral disease, partly because individual mice that appear healthy may introduce the infection to a susceptible colony, with devastating results. Mortality may exceed 90 percent in a severe outbreak. Sudden deaths, with mice showing swelling of the eyelids and scaly areas on the nose, are indicative of the disease. Any mice which do survive will be immune if they encounter the infection again later in life.

Unfortunately, when an outbreak does occur, no treatment is

available. In commercial colonies, vaccination is sometimes carried out on susceptible mice. This needs to be repeated twice a year, with the vaccine being administered at the base of the tail. The tissue is pricked and a drop of the vaccine applied. It is normal for a spot to occur where the inoculation has been made.

Sendai virus, which often leads to a fatal pneumonia, poses a serious threat to young mice and hamsters. Rats may carry this infection, but rarely show any clinical signs.

'Sialodacryoadenitis', a viral infection in rats, spreads rapidly through a colony, attacking the tear and salivary glands around the head, and causing swelling of these areas. The disease will often resolve itself and causes low mortality.

Disease in chinchillas
Chinchillas appear more at risk from bacterial ailments, rather than viruses. It is especially important with these valuable animals to seek veterinary advice. A post-mortem examination can identify a particular disease and will thereby help to prevent further losses.

Unfortunately, the symptoms can be variable. In the case of infections with the bacterium *Listeria monocytogenes*, for example, some animals may die suddenly with no obvious symptoms, whereas others may develop neurological signs beforehand, including paralysis of the hind limbs. In this instance, the veterinarian may recommend a course of antibiotics.

Below: *This chinchilla is having its teeth trimmed and filed back by a veterinarian. Overgrown incisor teeth can cause serious problems.*

Parasitic ailments

Parasites can be divided into two broad categories: those found externally on the surface of the body; and those that occur inside the animal.

External parasites In spite of their reputation, rats and other rodents rarely carry fleas. Indeed, they are more likely to be infested with lice. Like other skin parasites, lice can result in skin irritation and hair loss, with affected rodents seeking to reduce the irritation by rubbing their skin. Lice should be visible on close examination of the fur, using a magnifying glass.

Various types of mites have also been identified. Interestingly, some strains of rodents seem more susceptible than others, and male mice frequently develop more serious symptoms than their mates. Any unexplained hair loss with scabs tends to suggest external parasites.

Certain underlying diseases may encourage the development of a parasitic infection. Old hamsters suffering long-term kidney failure, for example, frequently show signs of *Demodex* mites along their backs, where hair loss is most obvious. These mites live in the hair follicles and are hard to remove.

The traditional remedy for combating external parasites is the careful use of a dichlorvos strip. Position this impregnated resin strip over the cage, but out of reach of the rodents. You can use it for up to three days at a time, repeated at fortnightly intervals over a period of six weeks or so.

If you suspect that your pet may be afflicted with external parasites, see your veterinarian. There is a new group of drugs, known as the ivermectins, which are very effective against most parasites. It may be possible for your veterinarian to treat a rodent directly by injecting one of these preparations.

Internal parasites A wide range of internal parasites has been reported, although they are generally of little significance to the

Above: *Mouse pox. The effects of this virus can range from a mild transitory infection to a fatal disease. Not common in pet mice.*

pet owner. Indeed, a number may be present in the animal's body and cause few, if any, symptoms. Typical examples are various blood parasites and certain intestinal worms.

Certain protozoa, microscopic unicellular organisms, can cause clinical signs of illness if they are present in the intestinal tract. The disease known as 'coccidosis' can result from infection with various protozoa. Newly weaned rodents are most likely to develop symptoms of coccidosis, typically diarrhoea.

The most serious protozoal parasite, simply because it can be spread to humans, is *Toxoplasma gondii*. This is, in fact, of greater significance in cats, which can become infected by catching infected mice. The life cycle can only be completed in the cat, but infection can be spread to mice and other rodents if cats have access to their food or bedding, contaminating it with the infective stage in the life cycle known as the oocyst. The symptoms in mice are variable, and may include abortion, since the protozoa can cross the placental barrier and infect developing foetuses. Spread to humans from mice is not likely since both are intermediate hosts, and are incapable of producing oocysts.

Chinchillas seem to be especially susceptible to the effects of toxoplasmosis, and an infection may prove fatal. While cats and

Above: *The dry, scabby skin of this hamster is a typical symptom of the fungal infection ringworm. Handle affected animals with care; the fungus can affect humans.*

Above: *Hair loss in a hamster, which may result from several conditions. Seek veterinary advice for a correct diagnosis. Older hamsters tend to lose their fur naturally.*

rodents should not be mixed in any event, you should also ensure that cats cannot gain access to rodents' bedding or bathing water, as this may lead to the transfer of infection.

Another protozoan that can cause losses amongst chinchillas is *Giardia*. Deaths can be sudden, or in some cases infected animals may have bouts of diarrhoea and constipation over a period of time. Since it is vital to diagnose this disease with certainty, arrange for a post-mortem examination to be carried out as soon as possible after death if *Giardia* is suspected.

Ringworm
Although it may sound like a parasite, ringworm is in fact a fungal disease. Various different fungi can give rise to clinical signs, most noticeably hair loss in a circular pattern. The centre of the lesion is dry and perhaps scabby. Treatment with the specific antibiotic griseofulvin is possible, but will be expensive and protracted, so affected stock is often painlessly destroyed. The disease is also transmissible to humans, causing reddish circular patches, notably on the forearms where the skin has come into contact with the animals.

If you suspect that your pet is suffering from ringworm, avoid handling it without a pair of disposable gloves, to minimize the risk of spreading the disease. You should also seek veterinary advice. In some cases, the ringworm lesion will show up as an apple-green fluorescence under a special light

known as a Wood's Lamp. Not all types do fluoresce in this way, however, so a sample culture – which may take several weeks to grow – may need to be tested to confirm the diagnosis.

Like other diseases, ringworm is particularly serious if you have a breeding group of rodents. The fungal spores are very resistant and can survive for long periods in the environment. Be sure to disinfect the accommodation and utensils thoroughly to prevent the disease spreading. Ask your veterinarian for advice about the most suitable brand of disinfectant for this purpose. Some disinfectants are likely to be toxic, especially those containing cresol compounds.

Fur-chewing
Ringworm in chinchillas should not be confused with the vice of fur-chewing. The reasons for this behaviour are not clear, but it is seen in other species as well. Typically, an animal chews the fur on its sides, creating short, virtually bald areas. If the hair loss is on the head, then another member of the group is likely to be responsible. Some strains of chinchilla appear to be more badly affected than others, although environmental factors may also have a bearing. A shortage of suitable material for the animals to chew on may be a contributory factor and it may be possible to bring about an improvement by providing more fresh hay. Over a period of time, the fur will regrow once the vice has been corrected.

Tumours

Rodents have a relatively high incidence of tumours. These are more likely to be seen in older animals, with malignant tumours affecting many of the internal organs as well as the skin. Clearly, the symptoms will vary according to the site of the tumour, but treatment is not really likely to be effective. If you suspect that your pet is declining over a period of time, consult a veterinarian, who will painlessly destroy the rodent if necessary to prevent suffering.

Slobbers

This description refers to the threads of saliva which appear around the mouth in rodents suffering from dental malocclusion, especially of the incisor teeth at the front of the mouth. In chinchillas particularly, it appears that this condition may be inherited and affected animals should not be used for breeding. Although it is possible to trim the teeth at regular intervals, this is best undertaken by a veterinarian. Take immediate action if you suspect this condition since the rodent will not be able to eat.

Other inherited problems

Selective breeding of livestock for traits considered desirable is almost certain to have unfortunate side-effects in a proportion of the population. This applies to rodents as much as to dogs or cats. Indeed, kinked tails resulting from genetic abnormalities are common in both mice and Siamese cats. While this will not have any effect on the life of

Below: *A chinchilla with slobbers – saliva dripping from the mouth. It usually indicates a dental problem, such as malocclusion of the teeth.*

a pet, affected stock should not be used for breeding purposes.

There are some neurological disorders, however, that are potentially more serious, and affected animals will have to be painlessly destroyed. Defective development in mice, usually of the inner ear, can cause circling behaviour, with these mice sometimes being described as 'whirlers'. Study has shown that such defects can be linked in some instances to coat colour. Another very similar problem – looping – results in affected mice jumping repeatedly in vertical loops. In the process they may injure themselves on the roof of their quarters.

It is not always known with certainty whether a genetic cause underlies abnormal behaviour, since the animals' environment may also be involved. Yet it seems that breeding with such stock leads to an increasing incidence of the particular complaint. This is certainly the case with whisker-biting in mice, which is a serious problem for exhibition stock. The whiskers themselves have a sensory function and must be present in mice being shown, otherwise they are disqualified. The mouse responsible in a group can usually be identified because its whiskers are intact. Rats may also be afflicted. Overcrowding can be a contributory factor, with the dominant individual in a group assaulting its companions in this way, rather than fighting overtly.

Fewer inherited weaknesses have been identified in other rodents, although it is known that inbred hamsters may suffer from hereditary cardiomyopathy, a condition in which the heart muscle literally wastes away. Losses from this condition are most likely when the young hamsters are about four months of age. Gerbils can suffer epileptic seizures, with some strains being much more at risk than others. Left quietly on its own for a short period, an affected rodent will usually recover without problems. Stress, caused by handling, can cause a relapse however.

Table of health problems

Signs of infection or abnormal behaviour	Possible causes	Action
Bleeding. Large areas of skin appear damaged.	Injuries caused by fighting, particularly during mating period.	Dab with antiseptic. For deep wounds/ abscesses consult a veterinarian.
Snuffling breathing. Possibly combined with neurological symptoms, e.g. loss of coordination and circling behaviour. Especially in rats and mice.	Murine respiratory mycoplasmosis, a mixed infection that spreads in overcrowded conditions. Build up of ammonia in dirty quarters makes respiratory tract more susceptible to infection.	Repeated antibiotic treatment prescribed by a veterinarian. Clean quarters thoroughly. Separate affected stock.
Diarrhoea ('Scour'). Loose droppings. Non-infectious.	Feeding excessive amounts of greenfood.	Limit quantities of greenfood.
Infectious causes. Animal typically adopts hunched posture and is reluctant to move. Fur in poor condition and held away from body.	Protozoal parasite causing coccidiosis.	Specific drugs from a veterinarian.
	A viral infection causing diarrhoea of infant mice. Intestinal function may be permanently impaired.	Antibiotic treatment may prevent secondary bacterial complications.
	Bacterial infection causing Tyzzer's Disease.	Prompt antibiotic treatment prescribed by a veterinarian. Quarantine new stock for two weeks before introducing animals to an established community.
Diarrhoea, loss of appetite followed by wasting. Affects hamsters only.	Bacterial infection causing 'wet tail'. Small intestine becomes inflamed and restricts passage of food through the gut.	Treatment may be possible but long-term damage to the small intestine is likely to have occurred. Disinfect quarters thoroughly after an outbreak and keep litters separate.
Periods of diarrhoea and constipation over a period of time in chinchillas. May also be a cause of sudden death.	Protozoan parasite: Giardia.	Specific drugs can be obtained from a veterinarian.
Variety of symptoms, including abortion in mice.	Protozoan parasite: Toxoplasma gondii. Can be spread by infected cats and passed to humans (by cats, not mice).	Keep cats away from rodents, their bedding and foodstuffs. Wear gloves when cleaning cages and dispose of litter carefully.
Paralysis of hind limbs. Sudden death.	Bacterial infection: Listeriosis.	Antibiotic treatment by a veterinarian if the condition is diagnosed early.

Signs of infection or abnormal behaviour	Possible causes	Action
Swelling of tear and salivary glands in rats.	Viral infection: sialodacryoadenitis.	The condition often clears up without special treatment.
Skin irritation, hair loss, scabs.	Lice and mites, such as *Demodex*, spread by contact with affected individuals and their surroundings.	Restricted use of a dichlorvos strip positioned over the cage. Injection of ivermectin by a veterinarian. Direct treatment may also be possible in some cases.
Hair loss in a circular pattern. Centre of lesion can be dry and scabby.	Fungal disease: ringworm. The spores can survive for long periods in the environment.	Antibiotic treatment prescribed by a veterinarian may be effective. Handle rodents with gloves to avoid infection of humans and to reduce spread among other rodents. Disinfect cages and feeding utensils.
Bald areas on the head or on the sides of the body.	Fur chewing, self inflicted or by one member of a group chewing the fur of others. Caused by environmental stress and/or lack of suitable material to chew.	Reduce overcrowding. Provide fresh hay. Must be distinguished from ringworm and the parasitic conditions listed above.
Whiskers bitten off.	Whisker biting. One or more rodents attack the others in a group. An inherited condition, but overcrowding can be a contributory factor.	Avoid overcrowding. Culprit can be identified as it will still possess a full set of whiskers.
Threads of saliva around the mouth.	Slobbers, caused by dental malocclusion, especially of the incisor teeth at the front of the mouth. Can be an inherited condition.	Have the teeth trimmed by a veterinarian, otherwise the affected animal cannot eat.
Genetic disorders: Whirling/looping. Circling behaviour. Jumping in vertical loops, often causing injury. Associated with mice.	Defective development of the inner ear. Inherited condition.	Do not use the animal for breeding.
Kinked tail.	Genetic abnormality.	Do not use the animal for breeding.
Epileptic seizure, most common in gerbils.	Inherited weakness, but can be aggravated by stress.	Leave rodent quietly on its own to recover. Avoid handling it too much.
Sudden death in hamsters around four months old.	Cardiomyopathy – degeneration of heart muscle. An inherited weakness.	Avoid in-breeding with susceptible stock.

The principles of genetics

Practical advice on breeding each group of small mammals follows in the appropriate sections of Part Two. As a prelude to those sections, here we look briefly at the basic principles of genetics, investigate some simple examples of genetics in action and discuss the need to keep accurate breeding records.

Basic genetics

Breeding fancy varieties of rodents for specific characters follows the same basic rules of genetics (the science of inheritance) that apply to the breeding of all animals and plants. In hamsters, gerbils and the other domesticated rodents, the most prized characters are the colour, length and texture of the fur, the eye colour, etc. If you are breeding animals to conform to set show standards then it is vital to understand how these characters are passed from generation to generation. If you are breeding purely for pets then you may not be so concerned about the outcome. Even so, you may wish to try for a certain result by pairing up animals with desirable features.

The basic rules of genetics were first laid down by Gregor Mendel, an Austrian monk who brought the analytical eye of a mathematician to the results of exhaustive experiments he carried out, initially with pea plants. Working in the mid-1800s, Mendel recorded the inheritance of simple characteristics from one generation to another and developed a series of statistical 'rules' on the basis of the outcome. It was not until the early 1900s that Mendel's pioneering work and the emerging science of cell biology were harnessed into a more complete understanding of the mechanism of inheritance. Even today, when electron microscopes can probe the inner secrets of the cell, Mendel's basic 'laws' of genetics still hold true.

What Mendel knew simply as 'inherited characters' we now know exist as genes on the thread-like chromosomes within the cell nucleus. Chromosomes occur in pairs, and these become separated

Parents

Homozygous Albino

This series of overlapping cards represents succeeding generations of hamsters and illustrates the basic principles of genetics in action – the so-called 'Mendelian ratios' based on the pioneering work of Gregor Mendel. The circles within each animal carry the genetic code for that physical character. Thus, pairing homozygous Golden and Albino hamsters produces 100% Golden/Albino in the first generation.

in the sex cells of the parents (sperm and eggs) and are recombined at conception. This splitting up and recombination process lies at the heart of genetic variation; quite simply, it allows the genetic 'cards' to be 're-shuffled' in each succeeding generation. As a result, the offspring receive genes from both their parents.

This does not mean that the offspring display a 'mixture' of their parents chracteristics. Quite the opposite, for some genes (and hence characteristics) are dominant over others and these alone may be evident in the physical appearance of the offspring. These two types of genes are called, quite simply, 'dominant' and 'recessive'.

There is an important distinction between the genetic make-up – the so-called genotype of an individual – and the outward expression of those genetic characteristics in terms of the physical appearance –

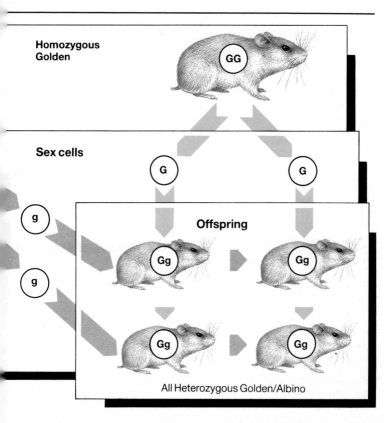

Homozygous Golden GG

Sex cells G G

g g

Offspring Gg Gg

Gg Gg

All Heterozygous Golden/Albino

the phenotype – of the individual. Thus, two individuals can have the same phenotype (appearance) but different genotypes (combinations of genes).

Where two identical genes for a certain character occur opposite one another on the paired chromosomes, such as two dominant or two recessive genes, the individual is called homozygous for that character. If the genes are different, i.e. one dominant and one recessive, the individual is heterozygous for that character. All this rather complex terminology will become clear in the following example.

Genetics in action
Pairing a Golden hamster with an Albino one demonstrates the principles of genetics in action. The golden character (i.e. one that causes the natural coat colour of the hamster) is dominant over the albino

(white) character. Thus, if you pair a homozygous Golden hamster – designated with the capital letters 'GG' to represent the two dominant genes – with a homozygous Albino hamster – for which 'gg' is used to represent the two recessive genes – all possible combinations produce a result of 'Gg' in the offspring. And, since the golden character dominates the albino one, the resulting offspring are all golden in colour but carry the albino characteristic in their heterozygous genotype. This is usually indicated with an oblique line, as follows: Golden/Albino.

On statistical grounds, pairing these heterozygous hamsters will produce litters with 25% homozygous Golden (GG), 50% heterozygous Golden/Albinos (Gg) and 25% homozygous Albino (gg). This is shown in the 'genetic cards' on the following page.

In reality, the results in one

37

particular litter may not correspond exactly to the expected ratios, since these are calculated as averages over a large number of individuals.

In some cases, more than one gene is involved in deciding a set of characteristics. The same basic principles of inheritance apply, however, and it is possible to arrange all the possible combinations of the genes concerned in a matrix as shown opposite and work out the expected results in the offspring. It is vital to know the genotype of the individuals concerned, of course, and to understand how the character is inherited.

It is also possible for different genes to occur at the same position, or locus, on the chromosome. This creates a range of effects, principally involving coloration. In mice, for example, the so-called Albino Locus may play host to several different genes. This produces a wide range of results, ranging from the normal colour through paler variants, such as the Himalayan, to the pure white, pink-eyed Albino form, in the homozygous state.

Sex-linked characters
The Golden/Albino genes featured in the previous example are located on the so-called 'autosomes' in the cell. These are the 'straightforward' chromosomes in the cell nucleus that do not determine the sex of the individual. The pair of sex chromosomes – labelled XX for female and XY for male – also carry genes that determine characteristics in the animal. Since the Y chromosome is shorter than the X chromosome, some genes carried on the X chromosome will not have corresponding ones on the Y chromosome. Thus, for any sex-linked mutation, the male's genotype will correspond to the phenotype.

Devising a breeding system
Although it is possible to produce a rodent that conforms very closely to the official show standard from a random pairing, repeated show

Parents

Heterozygous Golden/Albino

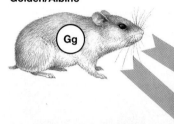

These 'genetic cards' carry the story into the second generation and show the predicted results of pairing heterozygous Golden/Albino hamsters. Presuming that all combinations of the sex cells are possible, the 'laws of inheritance' predict that 25% of the offspring will be homozygous Golden, 50% heterozygous Golden/Albino, and 25% homozygous Albino. This may not apply to every litter.

successes at the highest level rely on careful selection of stock and a meticulous breeding system. If this is your aim, visit as many shows as possible and study the entries in order to gain firsthand experience of what the judges are looking for. Official standards are useful guidelines, but they are no substitute for seeing and appreciating the strengths and weaknesses of the stock concerned.

In many cases, breeders resort to in-breeding to unify the favourable characteristics of their animals. This entails pairing closely related stock, such as father to daughter. It is not often recommended to pair brother to sister directly, however, since there is very little genetic variation in such situations. Always undertake in-breeding carefully, to avoid emphasizing the undesirable features at the same time. Remove poorly coloured individuals, for

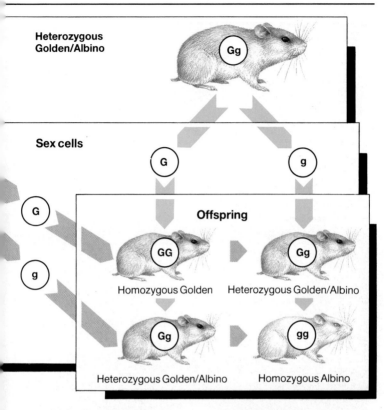

Heterozygous
Golden/Albino

Gg

Sex cells

G

g

G

g

Offspring

GG
Homozygous Golden

Gg
Heterozygous Golden/Albino

Gg
Heterozygous Golden/Albino

gg
Homozygous Albino

example, at every opportunity during such a breeding programme.

Line-breeding, a less rigorous form of in-breeding, entails the use of more distantly related animals. It can help to stabilize desirable traits within a given population, but in a less radical way than direct in-breeding.

New mutations are most likely to arise in closely related stock. This is not because of a specific weakness in the animals. It is simply that a recessive genetic mutation is more likely to show itself in the phenotype with closely related stock that could be carrying a mutation of this type in its genotype.

Whether you are breeding small mammals for colour, exhibition or simply for pleasure, it is vital to devise an adequate recording system, so that you can recognize and trace the offspring of any particular mating. This is obviously important for future pairings, but

accurate breeding records can also yield valuable data in the short term.

By studying the numbers of offspring produced by particular matings, it is possible to increase the overall reproductive potential of the stud by selecting young stock from the most prolific pairs for the breeding programme. Females that produce only small litters, for example, tend to pass on this trait. Directly as a result of this, the strain of Variegated Mice was lost after the Second World War.

Litter size is not entirely under genetic influence, however, as nutritional factors may also be involved. If the overall reproductive rate for the species concerned is poor, then you will need to examine the diet, and possibly raise the Vitamin E level; in some species, this has a direct bearing on fertility. Wheat germ oil, available from pet stores, is an excellent source of Vitamin E. (See also pages 24-27.)

Choosing a pet rodent can be difficult; there are so many colours available and, in some cases, differing coat types as well. Generally, however, the smaller rodents are not expensive and they are freely available, either from pet stores or from private breeders. Relatively few pet stores stock chinchillas, however, because they are significantly more expensive than the other species, but there are special farms which will supply stock direct to the public. If you are particularly interested in showing your pets at a later date, start by obtaining stock from an exhibitor. Various groups cater for those who keep and exhibit the rodents featured in this book. If you have difficulty in contacting a local club, seek out the national organisation, which should be able to direct you to a breeder in your area.

Since rodents generally have rather a short natural lifespan, try to obtain young stock. With careful handling, young animals should become very tame, whereas older rodents may be more reserved.

Before buying, always look carefully at the animals on offer. Note any that appear hunched up, with their fur fluffed out; this may indicate illness, or even maloccluded teeth. Avoid buying rodents showing any signs of hair loss, wounds or scabs. This could be linked either to parasitic disease, notably mange resulting from a mite infestation, or simply old age and bullying.

Do make a point of checking the sex of the animal. Although this is important from the breeding and compatibility point of view, it may not matter so much if you are seeking a single pet. You may prefer females in the case of rats and mice especially, however, since their urine is less strong smelling than that of their male counterparts, which can be an important consideration in the home. Single sex groups are recommended if you wish to keep more than one rodent in the same quarters; this will minimize the risk of fighting. Detailed advice on breeding is given in each section.

Gerbils

In this section we consider briefly how gerbils live in their natural environment and then turn our attention to keeping pet gerbils in captivity, with sections on handling, accommodation, breeding and colour forms.

Gerbils in nature

Gerbils form the subfamily Gerbillinae, a large group consisting of over eighty species. They have a wide range throughout most of Africa and parts of Europe, extending across Asia into Mongolia and China. Gerbils tend to live in arid areas, having adapted in several ways to the scarcity of water. By burrowing during the hottest part of the day, they protect themselves against dehydration. Then at night

Below: *Mongolian Gerbils. Well adapted to survive in an arid environment, they are relative newcomers as pets, although discovered in the mid-1800s.*

they venture forth to forage for seeds and similar foods that, in the rapidly falling temperatures, gain a covering of dew. This provides a vital source of fluid. Not surprisingly, the gerbil's digestive system is very effective at absorbing water and the kidneys are capable of producing a very concentrated urine, ensuring that water loss from the body is kept to a minimum.

The coat colour of gerbils reflects their natural environment. Those which live in sandy areas, for example, may have very pale coats. The furred tail does have a darker bushy tip, however, and this may serve to confuse predators. Rather like some lizards, gerbils can lose part of the tail and survive, although it will not regenerate. The tail is an important piece of their anatomy, however, since it helps to provide balance for the body when the gerbil is standing on its hind legs or jumping. Indeed, they can jump considerable distances, relying on

the powerful muscles at the top of their legs to provide the necessary impetus.

In common with other creatures that live in open country with little natural cover, gerbils have very acute hearing, in spite of their rather small ears. The bony capsule that encloses the middle ear is greatly enlarged, and serves to amplify even the smallest sound. Their sense of vision is equally well developed. The eyes are prominent and positioned so as to provide a wide field of vision and give them the ability to detect the slightest movement nearby.

Gerbils are social creatures, living in groups. For part of the day, they may even seal the entrances to their burrows. This helps to keep the internal temperature slightly lower, and may cause condensation of water droplets in the burrow. A typical colony may consist of up to three males and as many as seven females, with some juveniles co-existing in the group. They will forage collectively, digging if necessary for roots that can serve as an emergency supply of water.

Since an established group will not tolerate newcomers, it may

Above: *Always avoid holding a gerbil by the tip of its tail, since this will almost certainly cause injury. It is safe to use the base of the tail as shown here, however.*

seem that there would be a high degree of in-breeding within each colony, but studies of captive stock have revealed a unique system that avoids this need. Reproductively active females leave their colony and mate with a male of a neighbouring group, before returning to the established family colony to give birth and rear their offspring. Since many species of gerbils live in remote and inhospitable areas of the world, however, we still have much to learn about their natural lifestyles.

Handling pet gerbils

Gerbils prove ideal pets, especially for children. Unlike other rodents, they will rarely bite and are also far less susceptible to disease than mice, for example. They are not difficult to handle, but avoid grabbing the tail to restrain a gerbil; this will almost certainly cause injury. The best way of handling gerbils is to hold the base of the tail with one hand and grip the body with the other hand. Be careful, though, because gerbils are very nimble and will escape easily. Also avoid turning them on to their backs; they find this very distressing and will struggle accordingly. As a general rule, however, gerbils do not dislike being handled. They are naturally friendly and inquisitive by nature, especially once they are used to their owner and have settled in their quarters.

Accommodation and care
Gerbils will thrive in a converted aquarium, with a cover to prevent them jumping out. Give them plenty of suitable bedding so that they can excavate their own chambers. Room temperatures are fine for gerbils, and low humidity will not harm them. Indeed, high humidity will cause their fur to become matted, as described on page 12. You can incorporate a small nestbox in their quarters, where the gerbils may prefer to sleep. It is quite usual for them to undergo short sessions of frenetic activity and then suddenly sleep for periods.

Although gerbils drink little water in the wild, be sure to make water available to them in captivity. As a

guide, they will consume only about 4ml (0.2fl.oz) of fluid daily, and perhaps 8gm (0.3oz) of food. A diet based essentially on seeds or pellets suits them well, but avoid feeding excessive amounts of sunflower seed. Although gerbils are very fond of these seeds, their high fat content does lead to obesity if you feed large quantities of them. Offer a variety of greenfood.

Safe toys for gerbils include hollow tubes, which they can use as tunnels. Do not use playwheels, however, since these tend to be dangerous for gerbils. The tail is likely to become caught up, causing

the animal to become trapped or, worse still, to lose part of its tail. Since gerbils do not use their tails for climbing, unlike the prehensile tails of mice, they are more vulnerable to injury.

Breeding pet gerbils
Once they are about a month old, it is possible to distinguish male gerbils by the development of a scrotum, which appears initially as a dark area of skin near the base of the tail. In older gerbils, the testes are more evident in the scrotum. It is also possible to sex gerbils on the relative distance between the anus and the genital openings, as in other rodents. This is significantly longer in the case of males than females. The female's vagina is relatively close to the anus, whereas the male's penis is further away. When sexing gerbils, try to restrain them in the palm of one hand and use the other to lift the tail at its base. Supporting the body in this way will prevent the gerbil hanging free, which is very distressing.

Since they are social by nature, keep gerbils in small groups. For breeding purposes, start with young gerbils and introduce them to each other by the time they are two months old. A typical breeding colony consists of one male with two or three females.

Introducing adult gerbils to each other can be a fraught process and is likely to lead to fighting. Supervise any introductions carefully and, if fighting breaks out, separate the combatants using stout gloves. In the heat of battle, you are also likely to be bitten. You may have to repeat this process several times before the gerbils ultimately accept each other. As a last resort, rubbing talcum powder into the fur may serve to mask their scents and reduce the risk of spontaneous aggression. It is possible to use other substances, providing they

Left: *Young gerbils suckling. They will remain in the nest for about ten days. Gerbils, like most rodents, have proved prolific in captivity. They can be bred on a colony basis.*

are not harmful to the animals. Placing both gerbils in unfamiliar surroundings, such as a new cage, may also ease the introduction process.

Even with young gerbils, fighting normally breaks out very rapidly if the individuals are not compatible. After an initial few moments sniffing each other, they are likely to lock their teeth. After further contact, if the female starts moving around the male and then lies with her head slightly raised, showing her throat, it is likely that the pair will prove compatible. Once the gerbils are established, they will remain paired throughout their lives.

Gerbils normally reach maturity between the ages of two and three months. The reproductive period of heat in the female, known as the oestrus phase, lasts four days and occurs approximately every six days. Before mating, the male chases the female around the cage. She will then stand to enable mating to take place, which is a brief occurrence. The pair are likely to mate repeatedly over a short period, but they will not attempt to mate outside the oestrus phase.

The gestation period is approximately twenty-five days or shorter, although it can be slightly longer in some cases. Surprisingly,

the female will be ready to mate again within one day of giving birth. If the female does mate then, the implantation of the fertilized eggs into the wall of the uterus does not occur immediately, especially if a large litter has just been born. This effectively prolongs the gestation period to as long as forty-two days, with implantation occurring at about the same time as the first litter is being weaned.

The young gerbils, born blind and naked, remain in the nest until their eyes start to open at about ten days. They may inadvertently leave the nest earlier attached to their mother's nipple and will be returned by their parents. The male is also involved in looking after the litter.

The young gerbils develop quickly, with their fur appearing before they are a week old and their ears opening at a similar stage. Up to ten youngsters may be born in a single litter, although an average of between four and six is more likely. Gerbils are usually reliable parents. Occasionally, however, with a small litter of perhaps one or two, the female may kill her offspring, but such behaviour is quite rare in gerbils. Try not to disturb the nest, especially when the young are still helpless.

If you do have to handle any youngsters, take care not to transfer an unfamiliar scent to them, which in turn is likely to lead to them being ignored by their parents. This can be overcome by running litter from the

Below: *One-day old gerbils, handled purely for photography. They develop very quickly and some markings are already evident.*

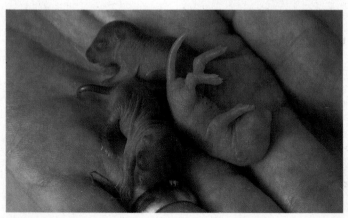

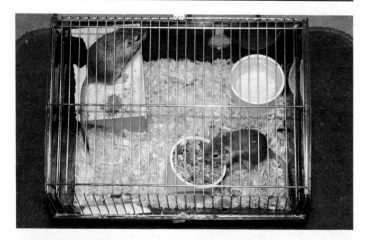

cage floor over your fingers beforehand. Take the same precautions when fostering young gerbils from one pair to another. It is best to remove the parents briefly, while placing newcomers alongside the original offspring to acquire their scent. It can be useful to sprinkle some wheatgerm over all the young gerbils at such times, which the mother in turn will clean off, reinforcing the scent marking on the newcomers in the process.

Gerbils normally start to eat independently from about two and a half weeks of age. Transfer them to separate accommodation at the age of three weeks, before their parents bear another litter. Keep a close watch on the youngsters at this stage to ensure that they are all eating without problems. Any which are not thriving will look unhappy and morose, being rather fluffed up in appearance. You may need to transfer such 'problem youngsters' back to their parents for a short time, although only as a last resort. In the normal course of events, transfer the young gerbils to individual sex groups when they are about four weeks old. Avoid keeping gerbils on their own if at all possible.

As with most rodents, the high reproductive capacity of gerbils can create problems, but you may find that a local pet store will take surplus stock, perhaps in exchange for foodstuffs or bedding materials. In order to avoid a population

Above: *Agouti gerbils feeding. Young gerbils start to feed on their own from about 17 days old and they can be weaned at 21 days.*

explosion, keep your gerbils in single sex groups. Gerbils will live for about three or four years on average, often succumbing to tumours in old age.

The Mongolian Gerbil

When people speak of a gerbil, they are almost certainly referring to the Mongolian Gerbil (*Meriones unguiculatus*). One of the fourteen species in the genus, all of which are sometimes described as 'jirds', the Mongolian reaches an overall length of about 20cm (8in). The domestication of the Mongolian Gerbil is a relatively recent event. Indeed, this species was not widely kept for study by scientists until the 1950s. It was found by a French missionary, Père David, who travelled extensively in Mongolia and China during the 1860s, and also made the Giant Panda known to the western world. Some wild-caught stock was sent to Japan and bred freely there. Mongolian Gerbils then passed to scientists in the United States, where Dr. Victor Schwentker was instrumental in establishing them. Their docile nature and ease of maintenance soon saw the popularity of these rodents spread beyond the confines of the laboratory.

Colour forms

Here we review briefly the main colour forms of gerbils. If your interest in gerbils broadens into the exhibition side, these notes will help you decide whether or not you have a potential prizewinner as a pet!

Agouti The normal colour form of the Mongolian Gerbil is described as the Agouti, golden brown with black ticking. The pale underparts have given rise to the alternative name of White-bellied Agouti. The pale fur may help to reflect heat from the ground in the wild. Good specimens should show a clear

division between the dark and pale areas of the coat. The black streak along the upper surface of the tail ends in a broader tuft.

The earliest mutation recorded in the Mongolian Gerbil, first known as the White Spot, originated in Canada towards the end of the 1960s. It proved difficult to establish, but has undergone a revival during recent years. As its name suggests, this mutation leads to the appearance of white spots in the darker coloured fur. Generally, such spots are clearest on the forehead and possibly on the nape of the neck. A few individuals also

have white patches on their tails as well. This feature has been transferred from the Agouti to other varieties, and may also be described as the Patched in such cases, where white markings extend over a wider area. In good exhibition stock, the white areas should be clearly delineated.

Pink-eyed White A predominantly white form of gerbil emerged in about 1968. With pink eyes and apparently no colour pigment present, it was initially regarded as an albino. Yet, in mature gerbils, some dark hairs become evident on the tail, typical of the Himalayan patterning seen in other rodents. Gerbils of this colour are now often described as Pink-eyed Whites. They have not proved to be as prolific as some varieties, and can be relatively slow to mature. A true Albino, i.e. one lacking any pigment whatsoever, has recently emerged.

Selective breeding in the UK has seen the development of the Dark-tailed White. At present in the hands

Left: **Agouti Gerbil**
This is the natural colour form of the Mongolian Gerbil, with a combination of black and brown hairs contributing to its appearance.

Below: **Black Patched Gerbil**
The white markings can be quite variable. In Black Gerbils, they tend to form distinct patches rather than spots, as in the original mutation.

49

of a very few breeders, this stock is closely related. Selection has been based on choosing individuals with the most prominent tail markings.

Black The Black form of the Mongolian Gerbil was first bred in the United States, at the USAF School of Aerospace Medicine in Texas. From here, stock was sent to Europe during 1978. The initial stock proved rather weak, however. Outcrosses were used to improve the overall vitality of this mutation, which is now well established. Like the original stock, however, most individuals still show traces of white hair. Virtually pure black gerbils are preferred for exhibition purposes.

Argente A British mutation that occurred at about the same time as the Black form has since undergone various changes in name, currently being referred to as the Argente, although perhaps the description of 'White-bellied Golden' conveys a more accurate impression of its appearance. Other names used include 'Cinnamon' and 'Golden', with the show standard calling for a pure golden gerbil free from any darker hairs on its upperparts and with a clearly delineated white belly.

Grey Agouti The Grey Agouti, or Chinchilla, mutation has had a chequered history. It appears to have emerged in about 1975, when a single male individual was discovered for sale in a London pet store, although the significance of this gerbil was not apparently realized by the staff. It went on to take the top award at the London Championship Show in that year, but died without breeding successfully. The mutation appeared lost, but then in 1980 a pair showing similar coloration was obtained from a laboratory source.

Right: **Pink-eyed White Gerbil**
Best described as a partial albino, this colour form of gerbil still retains some darker pigment, usually apparent along the tail. It is thus a typical example of the widely recognized Himalayan mutation.

Although paired together, no offspring were produced. To safeguard the mutation, however, each was paired to a Pink-eyed White. The youngsters were agouti in colour. When these were paired together, Grey Agouti offspring appeared in the litters.

Other colours Various colours have been bred from the primary

mutations. Pairing of Black and Argente gerbils saw the emergence of the Lilac, which is light grey in coloration with ruby red eyes. Occasional white areas are not unknown in the Lilac. The combination of the Lilac and the Pink-eyed White has given rise to the Dove, which resembles a very pale form of the Lilac. Similarly, the combination of the Pink-eyed White and the Argente has led to the appearance of the so-called Cream. Black and Grey Agouti forms have been used to produce the Blue, which in reality tends to be a dark grey in colour. Doubtless, new mutations will emerge in the future, and changes in coat length and texture, as have occurred in hamsters, may also become apparent in gerbils.

Above: **Black Gerbil**
This mutation emerged from two Agouti parents in the United States. It is hard to eliminate all white coloration: white areas are usually seen around the forelegs.

Other species of gerbil
From time to time, species other than the Mongolian are occasionally available, although they tend to be relatively expensive. The Egyptian Gerbil (*Gerbillus gerbillus*) is quite small, attaining a maximum head-to-tail size of about 12.5cm (5in). It is similar to the Mongolian species, but lacks the bushy tip to the tail, having only a sparse covering of fur on this part of its body. Coloration overall tends to be reddish, offset against white underparts. As before, keep these gerbils in groups, and they will develop a strong pair bond. They are easy to handle and care for, making ideal pets.

These features do not apply to the Indian Gerbil (*Tatera indica*), which is a relatively large species up to 43cm (17in) in overall length. It has

no fur on the pads of its feet, and this
has given rise to its alternative
description of Pink-footed Gerbil.
This is a gerbil for the specialist. To
breed Indian Gerbils successfully,
be sure to provide a nestbox in their
quarters, enabling the female to
retreat inside to have her litter.

Another large gerbil, with a body
length approaching 20cm (8in) and
a tail of similar size, is the Libyan
(*Meriones libycus*). Libyan Gerbils
resemble the Mongolian species in
terms of coloration, and are also
sometimes known as jirds. Their
gestation period tends to be
relatively long, extending up to thirty
days, with weaning taking place
when the youngsters are between
three and four weeks of age. Some
females will not tolerate any
interference when breeding,

Below: **Dark-tailed White Gerbil**
*Selective breeding using Pink-eyed
White Gerbils has given rise to this
distinctive form, in which the dark
coloration on the tail has been
developed into a prominent feature.*

Inset: Argente Gerbil
One of the more recent mutations, the Argente was first recorded in 1977. It has now been combined with other colours, such as the Pink-eyed White, to yield the Cream.

Above: **Lilac Gerbil**
This is a dilute form of the Black, and may show white patches, typically on the chest. The paler Dove form has arisen from crossings involving the Lilac and Pink-eyed White.

however, and so be sure to leave them undisturbed as far as possible once the young gerbils have been born. They also tend to be extremely destructive.

Other similar rodents
On occasions, other rodents with similar habits to gerbils are seen. The North American Kangaroo Rats, for example, are so-named because they tend to leap rather than run. They grow to an overall length of about 30cm (12in). They are not usually easy to tame, and prove aggressive to others of their kind. It is best to house them individually, therefore, in spacious surroundings and to offer them a similar diet to gerbils. They burrow extensively and are largely nocturnal, foraging for food above ground after dark. They store the food in cheek pouches and take it back into the burrow. Kangaroo Mice are smaller, being about 12.5cm (5in) overall, with half of this length being taken up by the tail.

Jerboas, which are also found in arid areas (including the Sahara Desert), have not gained the popularity of gerbils because of their more specialist requirements. (In the wild, they remain in sealed burrows during the day to conserve water.) They are also aggressive, and tend to bite without much provocation.

Below: **Blue Gerbil**
This new colour is not a primary mutation, but arose by crossing Blacks and Grey Agoutis.

Below right: **Grey Agouti Gerbil**
Also known as the Chinchilla from its colour; a genetically true Chinchilla Gerbil has yet to emerge.

Above: **Egyptian Gerbil**
This is one of the other species sometimes available. Colour mutations have yet to be recorded in these gerbils. They do not differ significantly in their needs from their better known Mongolian relative and make equally good pets.

Hamsters

These rodents are found in a wide range of habitats, from northern Europe in a broad band across much of Asia, apart from the southeastern corner. Twenty-four species are known but, as in the gerbils, only one – the Golden, or Syrian, Hamster (*Mesocricetus auratus*) – has become popular as a pet throughout the world.

The Golden, or Syrian, Hamster

The Golden Hamster was first discovered in 1839 and, forty years later, live specimens were brought to England from Syria by James Skene, who had been serving there in the diplomatic service. This group seems to have thrived for thirty years, with the final progeny dying in 1910.

Subsequently, there seems to have been none of these rodents in captivity until April, 1930. Indeed, it was suggested that the species was extinct, until Dr. Israel Aharoni discovered a nest of Syrian Hamsters on Mount Appo in Syria. The young hamsters were transferred to the Hebrew University at Jerusalem. The breeding programme was not entirely successful at first, since four of the eight hamsters escaped, and then a female died as a result of a fight with the only surviving male. From this unpromising beginning, however, the male mated successfully with both the other females and, within a year, three hundred and sixty-four offspring had been reared.

Above: *A sleeping hamster – quite distinct from the torpid state. Hibernation may occur in captive-bred stock; avoid triggering it with low temperatures and light levels.*

Some of the progeny were sent to Dr. Edward Hindle in England and, possibly via breeding stock at the London Zoo, Golden Hamsters became available to the pet-owning public. It was not until the start of the Second World War that these hamsters were seen alive in North America. It is amazing to reflect that all such hamsters kept throughout the world today are believed to be the direct descendants from that nest found on Mount Appo more than half a century ago.

Hibernation

An unusual and often disconcerting habit of hamsters is their ability to hibernate if environmental conditions are unfavourable. This is a natural trait, which to some extent is now less apparent in domesticated stock. The hamster's body temperature falls from the normal level of about 37°C (98.7°F) to a little above the environmental temperature. The respiratory rate is barely one breath a minute, whereas under normal circumstances the figure reaches up to one hundred or more. Since the heart beat can also be as low as four contractions per minute, compared with five hundred per minute in the active animal, to the casual observer a hibernating hamster appears dead. A fall in temperature, coupled with declining periods of light, will trigger hamsters to enter this torpid state.

Clearly, in a room in the home heated during cold weather, such behaviour is less likely to occur. To encourage a hibernating hamster to wake from its sleep, transfer it to a warm position where it can awake gradually. A temperature in excess of 20°C (68°F) is ideal. Gradually the hamster's breathing will become apparent, and its body will warm up as blood flow to the skin increases. If you discover a hamster apparently dead in the nest, treat it in this way to establish whether or not it has simply entered a torpid state.

Other factors also influence a hamster's readiness to enter a state of dormancy. These include the provision of a very deep layer of bedding material and, significantly,

Above: *The Golden Hamster, the most widely kept member of this group of rodents. All such hamsters in captivity have descended from just four Syrian individuals, although recently wild-caught ones have been seen in Europe. Hamsters are solitary by nature; keep them alone since they tend to prove highly aggressive to each other.*

an opportunity for the hamster to store food. Hoarding behaviour is quite natural, with food being taken back in the cheek pouches and stored in the nest.

Handling

While it is easy to handle a torpid hamster, this certainly does not apply to an untamed wide-awake individual. It is vital to encourage a young hamster to accept being picked up and handled without showing any signs of resentment. Once these rodents are used to the routine, it should be possible to lift them out of the cage and use both hands to form a restraining cup. Bear in mind, however, that hamsters can inflict a painful bite on the unwary. This can apply when feeding a small titbit, with the hamster wounding a finger by accident.

Although it is possible to wear gloves as a precaution, this may simply encourage the hamster to use its teeth at every opportunity, because it can be difficult to avoid hurting the creature while wearing 'insensitive' gloves. Physical contact with the warm surface of the skin tends to be more reassuring for

Below: *Avoid grabbing a hamster but encourage it to walk on your hands. Restrain difficult individuals by holding the skin over the neck.*

the hamster. You can restrain even a bad-tempered hamster quite adequately, though, by holding the loose folds of skin along the back, especially near the neck. Do not turn the animal over, however, as this will prove distressing.

Try to avoid hamsters becoming free in a room. Hamsters generally prove difficult to recapture once they have disappeared in a room because, unlike gerbils, they tend to be more timid and will retreat beneath floorboards if an opportunity occurs. Hunger may well encourage the rodent to emerge from its hiding place after dark, however, and you should then be able to recapture it safely. One particularly effective strategy involves using some books and a plastic bucket. Arrange the books so they form steps up to the top of the bucket; remove the handle of the bucket if necessary. Slice an apple and rub the cut moist surface on the books to leave a 'scent trail'. Place a thick layer of bedding at the base of the bucket and tip the cut apple on top. The hamster, attracted by the scent of the food, will climb up to the top edge of the bucket and should fall down inside, uninjured. If you have cats in the home, be sure to exclude them from the room in which your hamster is free until you have safely recaptured it.

Hamsters appear to have little

Above: *Although originating from an arid part of the world, hamsters will drink readily and should have water constantly available to them in a* *drinking bottle. An exercise wheel caters for their lively nature. They tend to be most active after dark, during the evening in a home.*

fear of heights, readily plummetting off the edge of a table, for example, possibly with fatal consequences. Whenever moving a hamster, therefore, do ensure that it is adequately supported should it begin to struggle. Do not frighten the animal unnecessarily by grabbing it while it is asleep, as distinct from being in a torpid condition, since this will intensify its natural dislike of being handled.

Accommodation and care
In the wild, hamsters tend to live on their own rather than in groups. They are not social by nature and so, apart from breeding purposes, it is best to house them on their own. Allow a minimum area of 625 sq.cm (100sq.in.) for each hamster (which grows up to 15cm (6in) in overall length); thus, the dimensions of their quarters should be at least 25cm (10in) square.

They will burrow into the floor of their cage, so provide a fairly deep layer of bedding material. Be sure that the bedding is not toxic or dangerous in any way. If eaten, unsuitable bedding can cause

impaction in the intestines, and this is likely to prove fatal. A metal cage will be strong enough to withstand the onslaught from the hamster's teeth, but over a period of time the urine is likely to attack the metal, causing bubbles of rust at first. This problem will not be encountered in a cage with a deep plastic base or in a plastic fish tank, but the claws of hamsters may scratch its sides.

Provide an exercise wheel for these active rodents, but be sure that it revolves smoothly, otherwise it will become a major source of irritation as it squeaks in the room. Hamsters tend to be nocturnal in their habits and, surprisingly, studies have shown that pregnant females are most active. They can 'travel' 8km (5miles) a day, walking on their wheel. Perhaps exercise improves muscle tone in preparation for birth, but even now little is known about the habits of hamsters in the wild.

Although diets prepared for other rodents suit hamsters well, their dietary needs are not yet fully understood. It appears that a protein level of about twenty-four

Above: *A Cinnamon Hamster suckling its young. Do not disturb them at this early stage; a first-time mother may be particularly nervous.*

percent is to be recommended, certainly during pregnancy. Interestingly, hamsters do seem to need fruits, especially apple, in their diet. Studies have suggested that hamsters fed on dried diets have smaller litters, with fewer ova actually implanting into the uterine wall. In addition, a higher incidence of cannibalism is likely in females deprived of fresh fruit. As a guide to food consumption, hamsters tend to eat about 15gm (0.5oz) daily, and can drink up to 20ml (0.7 fl.oz) of water, particularly when they are being fed exclusively on a dried diet. Be sure to remove any fresh food, however, before it can turn sour.

Breeding pet hamsters

Female Golden Hamsters are larger than males and, again, can be distinguished from males by the relatively short distance – under 2.5mm (0.1in) – between the anal and genital openings. The conformation of their hindquarters also tends to be more regular. Males have a noticeably longer ano-genital distance and a swelling at the base of their short tails, concealing the testes. They also lack the mammary glands present on the underside of females. There are normally seven pairs of teats in this species.

Breeding hamsters can be a costly undertaking, bearing in mind the additional accommodation required for the offspring. A litter may consist of up to sixteen youngsters, so be sure to find likely homes for surplus stock before pairing up the adults. Female hamsters mature early, by the age of a month in some cases, although it is best not to allow them to mate until they are about twelve weeks old. This will present difficulties if you have established a young pair.

It may be possible to keep a pair of hamsters together safely if they are housed in the same accommodation from weaning onwards. Otherwise, you will need to supervise mating. The larger female is likely to attack her prospective mate, especially if she is not ready to mate. Therefore, always introduce her to the male's cage, rather than the other way round. If the female is receptive, then mating will take place almost immediately, and then you can separate the hamsters again. Some breeders prefer to move both partners to new accommodation for mating purposes. If you opt for this scheme, move the male first so that he has an opportunity to settle down before introducing his prospective partner.

Oestrus in the hamster normally occurs in the evening, as befits a nocturnal species, with mature females cycling every four days. A receptive female will stand still with her tail held vertically, inviting the male to mate with her. This will last for just under half an hour. If mating is not successful, a sticky whitish discharge may be evident from the female's hindquarters shortly afterwards. This is quite normal and is not an indication of a uterine infection.

The developing ova will implant in the female's uterus about six days after mating, with the gestation period for the Golden Hamster lasting just sixteen days. Avoid handling the female during this period, although it may be preferable to transfer her to a converted fish tank where she can have her litter. This will ensure that

Breeding hamsters

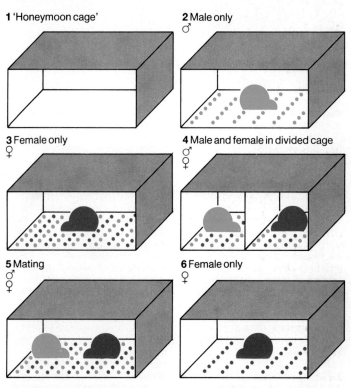

1 'Honeymoon cage'

2 Male only ♂

3 Female only ♀

4 Male and female in divided cage ♂ ♀

5 Mating ♂ ♀

6 Female only ♀

Above: *Breeding hamsters can be a fraught process and needs careful supervision. Transfer both prospective partners to the mating cage in turn, so that they leave their scents. Then set up a partition, with the hamsters on either side. Remove the partition, preferably in* *the evening, to allow the hamsters to meet directly. Keep a careful watch at this stage and separate the animals immediately if they fight. After mating has taken place, leave the female alone to have her litter or, alternatively, move her back to the original cage or plastic fish tank.*

Above: **Red-eyed Cream Hamster**
One of three recognized forms of the cream mutation, separated on the eye coloration. Coat colour varies from pale to deep cream.

none of the young hamsters can get caught between the bars when they leave the nest.

Under no circumstances keep the female hamster on a wire-mesh floor, as this will trigger cannibalism. Unfortunately, this vice is not uncommon in hamsters, and thus it is important to leave the female undisturbed in her nest. She is likely to be nervous, especially with her first litter. The average number of young hamsters, sometimes referred to as pups, is likely to be around seven. Large litters may be born slightly earlier.

The breeding cycle of hamsters ranks among the fastest of all mammals and, although naked and helpless at birth, the young pups will be capable of eating a proportion of solid food within a week. By this stage, it is usually safe to handle them, but take the precaution of rubbing cage litter on your hands to prevent transferring an unfamiliar

scent to their coats. Alternatively, use a blunt pencil that has been similarly treated to prise back the nesting material in order to glimpse the youngsters.

It is vital to supply fluid only in sealed drinking bottles, because once the young hamsters leave the nest they may become saturated or even drown in a full water bowl. As a rearing food, you can supplement the female's diet with wholemeal bread soaked in milk, but remember to provide this fresh each day in a clean container, because it will sour rapidly, particularly in hot weather.

The young hamsters are usually weaned at around three weeks of age, and it is certainly advisable to remove them from their mother by the time they are a month old, otherwise they may be attacked. After they are about six weeks old, the hamsters may start fighting each other and you will need to separate them. Young females can be easily distinguished by the teats, which are present from birth but become obscured by fur.

Unlike some other rodents, the adult female hamster does not come into heat immediately on giving birth, but is capable of mating again shortly after her pups have been weaned, or before this if they have died or been killed. Generally, however, it is preferable to wait for a short period to allow her to recover, especially if she has reared a large litter. The average female will breed during her first year or so. The maximum life expectancy for hamsters is about two years, although, occasionally, older individuals have been reported. Hair loss is common in hamsters towards the end of their lives.

Colours

The so-called Golden Hamster is in fact golden brown in colour, with whitish underparts. The grey underfur may exert an influence, especially on the paler belly colouring. A number of mutations and colour forms bred from primary mutations have been established and, at present, at least twenty-five such variants are known, along with three basic modifications to coat type: Long-haired, Satin, and Rex.

There is now so much scope for breeding hamsters that it is probably best to decide upon a particular type and develop from this, rather than pairing randomly in a mixed selection. If you intend to exhibit you will certainly need to specialize, unless you have unlimited time and facilities.

Black-eyed Cream Among the first mutations was the Black-eyed Cream. The depth of coloration does vary, however, and this is often a source of argument among exhibitors of the variety. There is a tendency for darker coloured apricot specimens to be favoured.

The Black-eyed Cream is described as a 'Self' mutation, which means that only cream coloration is permitted; any trace of white or other colours will lead to disqualification for exhibition purposes. Interestingly, the ear coloration of this variety can darken considerably, from a light grey in young animals through to black in older individuals.

Below: **Satin-coated Hamster**
There are various modifications to the coat type that can be combined with the different colours. The Satin feature produces a glossy coat.

Above: **Dark Golden Hamster**
This is darker in colour than the original Golden. There should be blackish circles around the eyes.

Below: **Normal Golden Hamster**
The natural form of Golden Hamster is actually brownish rather than golden. Eye coloration is black.

Ruby-eyed Cream The body coloration in this mutation is definitely lighter than in the Black-eyed variety, being almost pinkish cream rather than tending towards apricot. The ears are also paler, while the eye coloration, which is clearly reddish in young animals, darkens later in life. So much so that it may be necessary to look at the hamster in bright light to detect any trace of ruby coloration. Unfortunately, the Ruby-eyed Cream is not an easy variety to breed because, as in the case of other ruby-eyed mutations, adult males are sterile. This means that Ruby-eyed Cream females must be paired to normal-looking males known to be heterozygous for this recessive characteristic in order to obtain Ruby-eyed Creams of both sexes. (See page 36 for genetics.)

Red-eyed Cream The Red-eyed Cream is not afflicted with this problem, however, and has eyes that are clearly red. Two distinct forms are recognized, with the darker type having a coat colour resembling a shade of apricot,

Above:
Young male Yellow Hamsters
The yellow should be rich, offset against black ticking distributed evenly through the coat. Black eyes.

whereas the lighter variant is pale cream in colour. The ears are pinkish rather than grey.

Albino Ear coloration serves to distinguish the two recognized forms of the so-called Albino. Yet, since albinos by definition have no pigment present, only the Flesh-eared variety is a genuine albino. This form is pure white, with red eyes and pale pink ears, this colour being provided by the blood supply to the tissue. The Dark-eared form may tend to show a yellowish tinge to its coat and, interestingly, the ears do not darken until the animals are about twelve weeks old. The reddish eyes also darken with maturity. This form is best described as an incomplete albino, since it still possesses some pigment. It is a recessive characteristic, but will act in a dominant way when paired with its Red-eyed counterpart. There is

67

Above: **Dark (left) and Light Grey**
This photograph clearly shows the contrast between the two varieties; the Dark Grey is now most common.

Below: **Sepia Hamster**
This variety has had a chequered history; the original form bred from Golden stock is considered extinct.

Below: **Blond Hamster**
One of the new colours that appeared during the 1970s, the Blond is a paler form of the Honey.

also a similar form known as the Black-eyed White.

Golden Various modifications to the depth of coloration have occurred in the Golden Hamster, with the Light Golden being very pale in appearance. Conversely, the Dark Golden is mahogany-red in colour, with black guard hairs scattered through the coat. The lower parts are greyish and the ears are virtually black. The crescent markings on the sides of the head are white. There is also a form known as the White-bellied Golden that originated in the United States. This form is no longer favoured, since breeding it also leads to the production of white pups without eyes because of a so-called 'eyeless white gene'.

Cinnamon Cinnamon hamsters first appeared in the United States and reached Europe in 1958. Since then, they have become one of the most popular varieties, with their orange coat colour offset against a bluish grey undercoat. The distinctive cheek patches and ears are cinnamon, whereas the crescents are white. In most cases, the belly tends towards cream rather than pure white. A less distinctive form, known as the Cinnamon Fawn, has resulted from crosses between the Cinnamon and Ruby-eyed Fawn, which is itself very scarce today.

New colours

The 1970s saw the emergence of
some interesting new colours that
are now well established. The
Honey is essentially yellowish honey
in colour, with deep ruby eyes
resembling those of the Cinnamon.
A paler form, the Blond, has black
eyes. Grey hamsters are also
growing in popularity and, again,
dark and light forms are recognized.
The Dark Grey is presently the most
commonly seen of the two grey
forms, being dark grey overall, with
a slate-blue undercolour. The cheek
flashes should be black, offset
against pale grey crescents, making
this form probably the most striking
of the two.

The Dark Grey has featured in the
development of the Black during
recent years. At first, the Black
Hamster was developed by
combining the Black-eyed Cream
and the so-called 'sooty gene'. The
Cream ancestry in this bloodline has
meant that many such hamsters
have white patches on their chins.
This artificial form is likely to be
renamed the Sable – which is a
more accurate description in any
event – if a genuine black mutation
occurs in the future, as has already
happened in the gerbil. Combining
the Black (Sable) with the Rust,
which is similar to but darker than
the Cinnamon, has yielded the
Chocolate variety, which also tends

Above: **Tortoiseshell and White**
*Often described as the 'Tortie and
White'. The tortoiseshell character
is sex-linked in its inheritance.*

70

Below: **Smoke Pearl Hamster**
Another of the new colours, this may be confused with the Dark Grey, but lacks the clear cheek flashes.

Above: **Rust Banded Hamster**
Rust coloration is linked here with the Banded pattern. The coloured and white areas should be distinct.

Above:
Long-haired Black-eyed White
The coloration of these hamsters should be as white as possible, although some tend to be a very pale yellow. Pinkish ears ideal.

Below: **Satin Tortie and White**
The satin mutation causes the fur to have a polished appearance. Satins should not be mated together, in order to preserve the coat quality.

to have white markings on its lower parts. Here, again, serious breeders aim to produce a completely self-coloured form.

Among other new colours, the Lilac or Dove – pale grey with a pinkish tinge to its coat – is rapidly gaining in popularity. It has been developed using Dark Grey and Cinnamon stock. Another recent addition to the grey forms is the Smoke Pearl, which is pearl grey.

Coat markings

Apart from the Self varieties, there are three basic types of markings now recognized in exhibition circles: Tortoiseshell, Banded and Spotted.

Tortoiseshell The Tortoiseshell is probably the most popular coat marking. The patterning in this instance consists of large patches of white, yellow and coloured fur, which, in a well-marked individual,

Above:
Long-haired Red-eyed Cream
The long-hair characteristic has lead to such hamsters being known as 'teddies' in North America. Ear coloration can vary in this instance from grey to a pale flesh colour.

Below: **Dominant Spotted Golden**
This form is similar in appearance to the rare Piebald. The spotted form can be combined with any colour.

Above:
Sable Rex (left)/normal Sable
*These Black (Sable) hamsters show
the difference in coat texture
resulting from the rex mutation.
Thin, sparse coats are a major fault.*

Below: **Cinnamon Rex Hamster**
*The distinctive appearance of the
rex results in a reduction in length of
the guard hairs and whiskers. The
rex feature can also be bred with
long-haired and satin coat types.*

mode of inheritance. Thus, there is no likelihood of this characteristic appearing in the first generation, unless the other member of the pair is heterozygous, as explained in the genetics section on pages 36-8.

Coat types
Coat changes have also occurred in the Golden Hamster, so that the various colours can be combined with different coat types as well.

Long-haired/Angora The Long-haired, known in the United States as the Angora, is a striking mutation. It emerged in the USA during the 1970s and, initially, only males had the characteristically long coat. Even today, females tend to have a less profuse coat than males. Long-haired hamsters need special care to prevent their coats becoming matted. It is important to comb the hair gently so that it trails over the sides of the body. A thick coat is considered preferable, with self-coloured individuals being more impressive than their patterned counterparts.

are in equal proportions. Any colour, such as cream, can be introduced into the tortoiseshell pattern, with the ear and eye coloration conforming to this new colour. The tortoiseshell characteristic is sex-linked in its mode of inheritance (See page 38 for genetics.)

Banded Another accepted coat marking is the Banded, in which a white band around the body is combined with any colour. As in the Tortoiseshell, delineation between the white and coloured areas must be clear in a good exhibition specimen of a Banded hamster.

Spotted As in the gerbil, a Dominant Spotted form of the hamster is recognized. Ideally the spotted areas should predominate over the coloured markings on the coat. This characteristic can even be combined with the Banded. A very similar but genetically distinct mutation is the Piebald, which is recessive rather than dominant in its

Satin The Satin is the oldest of the coat types known in hamsters. The very glossy appearance of the coat can be quite striking. Avoid pairing Satins together, however, even if they are of different colours, since this produces offspring with thin hair. Paired to a normal-coated individual, this problem does not arise in the offspring.

Rex One of the problems associated with the Rex coat type has been a poor, sparse coat. This in turn has tended to detract from the development of this form. In the Rex the longer guard hairs present in the normal coat are reduced in length, causing the whole coat to appear rougher than usual. Rather than looking sleek, the texture of the coat resembles velvet. Even the whiskers of the Rex are short and rather curled in appearance. Again, this mutation can be combined with any colour, but shows to best effect when superimposed on Creams and other varieties with no undercoat.

Above: **Chinese Hamster**
The dark streak running along the back is a striking feature. This species is being bred successfully.

Below:
White-spot Chinese Hamster
This mutation in Chinese stock has a paler belly and distinctive spots.

Other species of hamster

The small Chinese Hamster (*Cricetus griseus*), growing to about 12.5cm (5in) in overall length, can be kept in groups, although females sometimes tend to be aggressive. Ideally, keep them in a converted fish tank, since they are sufficiently agile to escape from conventional cages. They need a similar diet to their Golden relative, but appear to require more greenstuff and fresh vegetables. Their gestation period appears to be about three weeks, with the youngsters becoming independent after a similar period of time. A White-spot mutation – a dominant trait – has just been recorded in this species.

Another small hamster occasionally available is the Dwarf Russian (*Phodopus sungoris*). In this species the male is usually

Above: **Russian/winter coat**
These hamsters can undergo a seasonal change in coloration, becoming much paler in the winter, which provides natural camouflage.

slightly bigger than the female. A satin mutation has been recorded in captive stock, while Russian Hamsters from the eastern part of their range naturally moult into a whitish coat at the onset of winter. In captivity, it is possible to induce this change by reducing light exposure. Care is similar to that needed by the Chinese Hamster, although the litter size tends to be smaller, rarely exceeding four or five pups.

Below: **Russian/normal coat**
This example shows the more common darker coat. It seems that coat colour can vary regionally.

Mice

To many people, mice are pests and carriers of disease. Fancy mice, which have been selectively bred over countless generations for more than a century, have an undoubted natural charm. The versatility of the mouse, which in the wild gave rise to so-called 'super mice' able to combat anticoagulant poisons by genetic development, is equally reflected in the domesticated strains. There are now well over fifty colour forms available, and modifications to coat type and length are also well recognized.

Handling

Mice are not difficult creatures to handle. To pick them up, use the base of the tail, holding it firmly between the thumb and forefinger. The tip of the tail is easily damaged, however, so do not handle it in this way. Once tame, there will be little need to lift a mouse by this means, since it will simply sit on the hand with a little encouragement. Alternatively, move a mouse by persuading it to enter a hollow tube of appropriate diameter and simply enclosing the ends with your hands. Never grip a mouse tightly when holding it, as this can cause serious internal injuries.

Below: *Mice are generally docile and can simply be restrained in the hand. Do not grip them tightly as this will cause them discomfort.*

Accommodation and care

Fancy mice are easy to cater for and social by nature, living contentedly in groups, although they can also be kept on their own. Do not keep male mice, or 'bucks', together since the smell usually associated with mice will become all too apparent; the mice use this strong odour for scent marking. Females, or 'does', rarely have any noticeable smell attached to their quarters, especially if you keep them clean.

It is possible to keep mice in a wide variety of enclosures, even hamster cages, but do not mix these two rodents together. Mice will be perfectly happy with a relatively shallow layer of litter, since they are not great burrowers. Be sure to provide hiding places and adequate bedding to form a nest, however. They will readily use a playwheel in their quarters.

Remember that mice will gnaw, and therefore wooden quarters are unsuitable for this reason. In addition, the urine of males will be absorbed by wood, causing a lingering odour, even if the cage is cleaned regularly. Under general circumstances, clean the quarters once a week, as for other rodents.

Feeding mice presents no problems, and the basic diet outlined on page 24 will suit them well. Also include some fresh items, such as apple and carrot, in their diet. They will also appreciate other

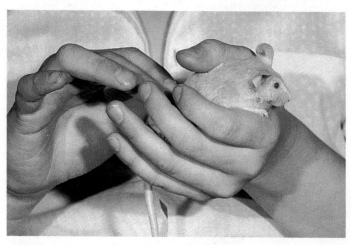

foods, such as small pieces of cheese, and these are useful for taming purposes. Offer a long thin slice of cheese rather than a cube, since the mouse will probably be less reluctant to take a strip, as this involves a less close approach to your outstretched hand. This will also minimize the risk of being bitten accidentally. Never forget to provide water, ideally in a sealed drinking bottle, and change this each day so that a fresh supply is always available. Also remove any uneaten fresh foods every day.

Many people like to allow their pet mouse out of its quarters, once it is fairly tame. This is fine, but do not forget to exlude cats and dogs from the room beforehand. Always stay with your pet to prevent it getting lost in the room; it can quickly disappear from view, possibly going under furniture or even beneath the floorboards if there is a suitable gap. As with hamsters, however, the mouse should emerge in search of food and it is worth trying the catching strategy described on page 60. Also, leave the mouse's quarters open; it may return of its own volition. Alternatively, try one of the traps available for catching mice alive; these may be useful for trapping an errant pet relatively quickly and without injury.

Breeding fancy mice
In a litter of mice, males tend to grow more rapidly, but this is not necessarily a reliable guide for sexing purposes. Again, the ano-genital distance is significant, with the gap being longer in males. Furthermore, apart from this comparative method, only females have two parallel rows of nipples visible along the abdomen. You may need to part the fur to find these.

Mice can mature very rapidly, being capable of breeding successfully when only five or six weeks old in some cases. Most breeders keep the sexes apart, however, until bucks are at least ten weeks old. Once the mice are introduced to each other, mating often takes place rapidly.

Females cycle at about five-day

Above: *An Albino mouse at home in a pocket. Even before the foundation of the modern Mouse Fancy, white mice were known and became popular, partly because of their clean appearance.*

intervals, and the resulting young are born within three weeks of mating. Pregnant does show a significant increase in size by the fourteenth day, and it is vital not to handle them unnecessarily from this stage onwards. Ideally, transfer the buck to separate quarters after mating, but the does will give birth quite readily in a group, even sharing the task of suckling their offspring among group members.

An average litter consists of about nine offspring, although double this number is not unknown. If all appears to be going well, do not disturb the female during the early stages after she has given birth. It is possible to see the first signs of pigmentation in the pups by the time they are about three days old, with fur finally emerging when the young mice are about a week old. By this time, their ears are developing well, and the eyes open by the fourteenth day. At this point they will start to show an interest in solid food. Within a further week or so the mice will be independent and you should transfer them to separate quarters.

Early removal of the buck prevents further mating immediately after the birth of the first litter. Most studs tend to have fewer bucks than does, partly because bucks will often fight each other if they have not been reared together. It is always safer to introduce mice on

Above: *Mice breed freely, with a gestation period of about 21 days. If breeding is not desired they should be kept in single sex groups.*

neutral territory, such as in new quarters, to minimize the risk of aggression being shown towards a newcomer in an established colony.

The majority of does will breed most prolifically during their first year, but some will breed well after this time. The average lifespan appears to be about two years, although this varies according to the strain concerned and possibly their management. A few individuals have lived for five years, but this is most unusual. After a year, there is a significantly increased risk of mice succumbing to various tumours. Always watch older stock carefully for telltale signs of tumours, such as gradual loss of overall condition and possibly unexplained swellings developing over the body surface. (See also Health care page 33.)

Below: *Mice litters can be very large; around ten offspring, or pups, is not unusual. Since this can place severe demands on the available housing, be sure to plan ahead. Your petshop may take any surplus.*

Above: **Self Chocolate Mouse**
This is one of the well-established Self varieties of mice. As with all selfs, the colour should be even; darker shades are preferred.

Below: **Self Dove Mouse**
Occasionally known as the Lilac, the name is derived from the overall grey tone. This form has been developed from Black, with the pink-eyed characteristic added.

Colours and coat variants
In view of the large number of varieties that have now been developed, fancy mice are initially categorized into one of five groups: Self; Tans; Marked Varieties; Any Other Variety; and Satins.

Self varieties
The Self group features mice with one coat colour only. Basically, ten distinctive colours are included in

Above: **Black-eyed White Mouse**
Two forms are recognized, with either red or black eyes. In each case, there should be no yellow.

Left: **Self Fawn Mouse**
Another of the pink-eyed varieties, which arose during the early 1900s. The coloration should be a deep tan.

this section. For exhibition purposes, the coloration is of prime concern to judges; it should be even and solid, showing no traces of other colours. Type, meaning the physical appearance of the mouse, accounts for the remainder of the points that judges can award.

The Self Black is a very old variety, known in Japan in fancy mouse circles as long ago as the middle of the seventeenth century. It is possible to breed this colour by using Self Blue and Self Chocolate matings, or Self Blue with Self Dove and other similar combinations, but the resulting black offspring may be of poor quality, with paler bellies often being a major flaw. The Self Blue is slate-blue in colour, although the depth of coloration does vary. It was first seen at a show in 1898, being bred in the UK by a Gloucestershire fancier, whereas the Self Chocolate is considerably

older. Darker individuals resembling plain chocolate in colour are considered preferable.

Pink-eyed varieties of both the Self Blue and Self Chocolate show paler coloration overall, being recognized separately as Self Silver and Self Champagne respectively. The gene responsible for pink-eye colour also led to the development of the Self Fawn, with pink rather than black eyes, and also to the Self Dove, which is dove grey in coloration. This variety is occasionally known as the Lilac.

While all the above colours belong to the so-called Black Group, the remaining colours in the Self category are linked under the red (or, more accurately, dominant yellow) gene heading. The Self Red was initially known as the Fawn, and is another old variety. It should be a rich, deep red colour overall. There are problems associated with breeding these mice, however, since the gene responsible is sublethal, resulting in small litters, with the mice themselves being prone to obesity. Therefore, avoid giving Self Red mice fattening foods, such as sunflower seeds and cheese. Since fertility declines in overweight animals, it is best to undertake early breeding in these

Above: **Dove Tan Mouse**
Now often hard to distinguish from the similar Silver Tan, this variety is quite variable in appearance. Like the Self Dove, this has pink eyes.

mice. Outcrossing, typically using Cinnamons, can help to overcome such difficulties but, obviously, fewer Self Reds will result.

The description of Fawn was transferred to the pink-eyed form of the Self Red, which was developed early in the twentieth century. Fanciers were experimenting, using Japanese Waltzing Mice (*Mus musculus wagneri*), which had pink eyes and were a subspecies of the forerunner of the fancy mouse, known as the House Mouse. These pairings transferred the pink-eyed characteristic to various strains and colours of fancy mice.

In the Self group, it is now permissible to exhibit Whites, Silvers and Creams with either pink or black eyes. The Pink-eyed White is essentially an albino but, although formerly very popular, it is less commonly seen today. This is possibly because the exhibition

standard demands a pure white coloration, whereas in reality most individuals have a pale yellow tinge to their fur. It is possible to breed selectively for pure white coats, but some exhibitors also resort to using a white powder in order to improve the appearance of their mice still further. In most litters you can expect some marked offspring, making this variety difficult to breed in large numbers.

The Pink-eyed Cream has virtually disappeared. The Black-eyed Cream, however, is still seen regularly, although it has been modified down the years. At first, it was bred from red stock selectively chosen for paleness of coat colour. Then a change occurred during the 1930s with the emergence of the Chinchilla mutation. Breeders were able to create Black-eyed Creams by combining the red and chinchilla features, with the latter exerting a diluting effect on the former, producing a pale body colour. Yet again, the problems associated with the Self Red, in terms of litter size and obesity, became apparent in the Black-eyed Cream, so another option was pursued to generate this colour. By developing Black-eyed Creams from Lilacs, such problems were avoided, but the complex pairings involved took place over six generations, with only a one in sixteen chance of finally producing a Black-eyed Cream.

Tans

Tans resemble selfs when viewed from above and can be bred in most of these colours; the difference lies in the fact that the underparts of the body are clear tan. Good exhibition specimens show a distinct division between the markings, with no overlap of the colours. Tans were first bred during the early 1900s and have since become very popular. The most common flaw in exhibition stock is the presence of tan feet. Another problem is that pairing the darkest tans together tends to produce tan coloration over parts of the body where it is not required.

Probably the most striking member of this group is the Black Tan, which has darker coloration on its lower parts than other members of the group. This contrasts with the Blue Tan, in which the tan marking is

Below: **Champagne Tan Mouse**
First bred during the 1920s, this has remained one of the most popular tans. Obtaining the balance between the tan underparts and champagne top colour is not easy.

extremely pale, being diluted to light buff. Chocolate Tans should be as deep in overall coloration as possible. In combination with the Dove Tan, the Chocolate has been used to develop the Champagne Tan. Alternatively, a Silver Tan can be used in place of the Dove Tan, since these two varieties are very similar. Indeed, it can be difficult to distinguish them.

It is not possible to breed Red or Fawn Tans, however, simply because their underparts are already tan in colour. Apart from the Tan varieties already listed, others may be seen occasionally. These include a Cinnamon form, which can be produced by crossing a Chocolate Tan with a Cinnamon. The Agouti Tan results from pairing a Black Tan with an Agouti, with this latter variety being featured in the Any Other Variety (A.O.V.) group for exhibition purposes (see page 90).

Marked varieties

These are essentially piebald mice showing different types of markings which are categorized accordingly. In spite of their widespread popularity, these are difficult subjects to breed for exhibition purposes, since the standards for the different markings can prove very demanding, with many individuals having to be discarded from the breeding programme as a result. It is possible to recognize the

pattern of markings in the nest, however, once the fur becomes apparent when the young mice are only a few days old. Most serious breeders will cull poorly marked specimens at this stage rather than rear them to maturity, although a local pet store may take such offspring providing they are otherwise sound.

The effects of concentrating on the coat markings so heavily are apparent in the exhibition arena;

members of this group are often relatively small and lacking in stamina. This is caused by the repeated in-breeding frequently practised in order to consolidate the strengths of a well-marked individual. The difficulties in breeding a good exhibition specimen have made stock of marked varieties correspondingly expensive, compared with self varieties, for example. The following forms fall within the Marked group.

Above: **Black Tan Mouse**
This variety is the original ancestor of all tans. Bred during 1896, it was used to develop both Chocolate and Blue Tans in the early 1900s.

Left: **Even-marked Mouse**
A black-and-white, genetically a pied. This is not an easy variety to breed for showing, as a significant percentage of the offspring do not show the desired pattern.

Below: **Broken-marked Mouse**
The markings in this instance should be of equal size, contrasting with the Even-marked variety shown at left. A testing exhibition subject.

Dutch The most sought after of the mice in the Marked group are undoubtedly the Dutch, which should show symmetry of markings on the head and a clearly delineated band of white and darker fur. The darker fur, described as the saddle, should extend from the tail to at least half way along the body. Pink or black-eyed forms are acceptable, in conjunction with a recognized colour. This can be a problematical variety to breed to the established standards. It can be difficult to ensure that the saddle extends far enough forward, for example, and excessive concentration on the pattern of markings required can

Above: **Himalayan Mouse**
*This can have either red or black
eyes, with a white body and coloured
'points'. Recorded also in the wild on
the island of Spiekeroog, Germany.*

lead to mice of poor type being
inadvertently bred. The Dutch is a
recessive character and, as a result,
breeding involves pairing closely
related stock.

Broken-marked By comparison,
the distribution of colour in the
Broken-marked form may appear
easy to achieve, since it is entirely
random. The problem in this
instance is to breed mice with equal
patches of white and coloured areas
over the body. There should be at
least eight patches – possibly more
– and they must be distinct and not
overlapping in a good specimen.
The only prescribed patch or spot

that must be present is located in
the nasal region, extending to one
side of the nose. To correspond with
this spot, the opposite ear should be
either white or coloured, being the
reverse of the patch. Indeed, the
ears should be odd-coloured as a
general rule. Dutch markings of any
kind should not appear on a Broken-
marked individual. Although
breeding this variety for exhibition
purposes can be very frustrating, a
well-marked individual has a
potentially long winning career on
the show bench.

Even-marked The Even-marked
variety is very similar to the Broken-
marked – and also dates back to
before the Mouse Fancy became
organized in 1895 – except that the
standard does not require the
patches and spots to be of
matching size. The ears in this case

are of the same, rather than differing colours, with even markings being favoured, creating a more symmetrical appearance than in the Broken-marked. Indeed, it can be said that the faults of one variety are the strengths of the other.

For a period, such mice were regarded as poorly marked Dutch or Broken-marked individuals, but they are now duly recognized as a variety in their own right. At present, few breeders concentrate their efforts on these mice.

Variegated Variegated mice do not show any individual marks, but should have colour distributed evenly over their body. Although derived from a wild-caught buck in 1897, the original strain of Variegated mice declined because of poor fertility and was ultimately lost during the 1950s. The major difficulty with breeding them successfully is to ensure that patches of solid coloration do not occur, notably on the head and at the base of the tail.

Rumpwhite The Rumpwhite, as its name suggests, can be bred in any recognized colour, with a white area of fur confined to the rump area alone. It is a dominant trait, so that the mating of one Rumpwhite to a Self will yield a complete litter of offspring with white rumps in the first generation. The pairing of Rumpwhites together is not recommended, however, since homozygous Rumpwhites are not viable, being affected by a lethal gene. Apart from this fault, the Rumpwhite is an easy mutation to establish and develop for show purposes, compared with other members of the Marked group. A good specimen will show a clearly defined pure white rump with no overlap of colour into the area.

Himalayan It was not until 1970 that the Himalayan form was finally recognized for exhibition purposes, although it may well have been bred first in about 1921 in the United States. Modern strains are of laboratory origin, but are now widely established in show circles. Officially the ideal pattern should conform as closely as possible to the markings of the Himalayan Rabbit, showing coloured extremities – nose, feet, ears and tail – while the body coloration should be pure white. At present, only pale chocolate points are known, but in time other colours may emerge, as has happened, for example, in the case of Himalayan cats.

Unlike other mice in the Marked grouping, good Himalayans are not difficult to breed. As is usual with

Below: **Rumpwhite Mouse**
This is one of the newer mutations, recognized with a show standard in 1972. Do not pair Rumpwhites together, because of a lethal gene.

Above: **Agouti Mouse**
Sometimes known as the normal,
since the coat corresponds to that
of the fancy mouse's ancestors.

this mutation, the depth of coloration of the points in influenced by the environmental temperature. Under relatively cool conditions, for example, the chocolate coloration becomes darker. The Seal Point Siamese is very similar to the Himalayan but has a beige body coloration, with brown seal-coloured points.

Tricoloured Tricoloured mice are considered the most desirable, as well as being the rarest. They have been known sporadically since the early days of the Mouse Fancy, but have never been established entirely successfully. The aim is to produce mice showing three different colours on their bodies. Work in this field has recently centred on the use of laboratory mice; unfortunately, these exhibit evidence of the so-called Varitint-Waddler gene in their genotype. As a result, the development of the

inner ear is affected, to the extent that severe neurological disturbances, such as waltzing, are evident in the stock. Careful breeding is required to eliminate such weaknesses.

Any Other Variety (A.O.V.) Rare varieties also make up the fourth group, known as 'Any Other Variety'. As with other colours, you may need to contact a specialist breeder to obtain such stock, although pet stores may occasionally have mice of these varieties available or be able to obtain them to order.
  Prominent among Any Other Varieties is the Agouti, which is basically brown or golden with darker markings in its fur in the form of ticking throughout the coat. The Cinnamon is similar, but can be easily distinguished by its brown rather than black ticking. A number of other varieties in this category are also ticked, including the Chinchilla, which has been used in the development of many other mutations. It is very similar in coloration to the Chinchilla itself

Combining Chinchillas and Golden Agoutis has led to the development of the Silver Agouti, although this variety remains quite scarce. Coloration is considered very important in these mice; there should be no trace of bronze apparent in the coat, for example. The Silver gene has been incorporated into other varieties, such as the Silver Grey, which is recognized in three shades, ranging from light through medium to dark. Even depth of coloration is essential in this variety. Rare but related forms are the Silver Brown and the Silver Fawn.

The Silver Grey may also have been used in the development of the colour now known as the Pearl, which was initially known as the Chinchilla before being standardized under its present name in 1933. The undercoat of Pearl mice is whitish, not white as in the case of the Silver Grey, with the individual hairs being tipped with black or grey at their ends. An even depth of coloration is preferred.

(see page 106), being bluish grey in overall appearance. A brownish tinge to the fur of a Chinchilla mouse is a serious fault, while its belly should be white. This variety seems to be prone to excessive moulting, however, which will spoil its appearance for exhibition purposes. Try to keep these mice in a controlled environment at an even temperature with a regular pattern of lighting to minimize this problem.

The pink-eyed mutation is also represented in the A.O.V. group, with the Argente being one of the most popular varieties in its category. The name 'Argente' is taken from the French word for

Below: **Argente Mouse**
This is the dilute or pink-eyed form of the Agouti, and similarly has been developed in other colours.

silver. It results from the introduction of the pink-eyed characteristic to Golden Agouti stock. As a result, the overall colour of these mice tends to darken with age, with the silver patterning becoming less evident in such cases. A similar mutation, the Argente Cream, is effectively the pink-eyed counterpart of the Chinchilla, showing the paler body coloration typically associated with this eye coloration.

An old variety which still features in the A.O.V. group is the Sable, developed by Walter Maxey in the 1880s. Today, only the dark coloration is acceptable, but formerly various shades were recognized. It is closely related to the Self Red, and indeed, the same breed weaknesses are apparent in the Sable, which may account for a relative lack of interest in this variety. Pairing a Self Red buck with Black Tan does will yield a proportion of Sables in the first generation. A good coloured Sable

is a rich, dark brown with a golden tan belly. The most common flaw in exhibition specimens is a pale nose.

Combination of Sable and Chinchilla blood has in turn given rise to the Marten Sable, which has a white belly. It is a scarce variety at present, but can be bred over three generations from Black Fox and Sable parents. The Black Fox itself has black upperparts and a pure

Below: Red Satin Mouse
This mutation, giving a silky sheen to the coat, can be combined with any colour or pattern. Very popular.

Above: **Chocolate Fox Mouse**
This is a member of the Silver Fox Group (named after the rabbit), which also includes Blue and Black.

white belly. This is categorized under the Silver Fox heading, along with blue and chocolate forms.

Satins
The rise of the Satin-coated Mouse has been quite spectacular. The origins of this mouse date back only to about 1955, yet now there is a separate section for them. It has proved to be a recessive characteristic and has been combined with a wide range of colours. Some colours can be linked more effectively than others with this trait, however, which provides a smooth coat with a satin finish. Those of the Red group look especially striking in a satin form.

Other coat types
There are only three further coat types in addition to the normal and Satin; these are: Astrex, Rex and Long-haired.

The Astrex is the oldest of these forms, being officially accepted in 1936. It is in effect a rex mutation, causing the hair and whiskers to be curled. Unfortunately, this feature is most apparent in young mice, with the curls giving way to waves by the

time they are about two months old. In older animals, the coat may be almost indistinguishable from a normal-coated mouse. Although this recessive character can be combined with any colour, this has done little to assure its popularity.

Confusion arose during the 1970s when a mutation known as the Rex appeared, bearing some similarity to the Astrex. As in Rex cats, for example, the coat of Rex mice is rather thin yet strongly curled. This mutation combined with the Self Black produces one of the most striking effects, if only because the melanin pigment in the mouse's skin obscures any areas of sparse hair.

The Long-haired mutation, also a recessive characteristic, became known in about 1966. In good specimens the coat overall should be long and silky. Again, young mice make the best subjects for exhibition purposes, with Pink-eyed Whites being most common, although other colours can be combined with this mutation.

In spite of all the colours now in existence, there is still scope for further development within the Mouse Fancy. Certainly, a free-breeding strain of Tricolours would enjoy strong support. An Abyssinian form, with a coat pattern in the form of rosettes as in the guinea pig of this type, would be popular.

Rats

Fancy Rats have never achieved the popularity of mice. Indeed, their following declined quite sharply from the late 1920s onwards, but has since revived, especially during recent years.

The development of Fancy Rats

Two species of rat were involved in the development of the fancy varieties: the Brown Rat and the Black Rat. The dominant influence has been the Brown Rat (*Rattus norvegicus*), which is believed to have originated in Asia and spread into Europe by the eighteenth century. It tended to displace the Black Rat (*R.rattus*), which is both smaller and less aggressive.

The original stimulus for rat breeding may have been simply to supply adequate quantities of animals for ratting contests in the early 1800s. In such contests, dogs, notably terrier breeds, were required to kill the largest number of rats in a given period of time. One Manchester Terrier of the period is said to have disposed of more than one hundred rats in just over six minutes, so a good supply would have been needed!

Rats were also being used for scientific studies towards the end of the nineteenth century and, almost certainly, it would not have been long before mutations started to appear in the offspring of captive-bred stock. Today, rats are widely used in various areas of research, with specific recognized strains available. These are preferred not primarily on the basis of colour, but on known genetic susceptibilities to medical problems, such as obesity.

Fancy Rats developed by selective breeding are exhibited in cages similar to those used for mice and judged to official standards for the variety concerned. While rats available from a pet store may not be suitable for exhibition purposes, they will provide a fascinating insight into the lives of these rather maligned creatures.

Below: *The Brown Rat, generally accepted as the original ancestor of today's fancy breeds. Rat fancying began in earnest in the late 1800s.*

Handling

Handle rats in a similar way to mice, but remember that rats are larger and can inflict a correspondingly more damaging bite. Try to avoid using gloves for handling purposes, since the rat tends to respond favourably to the warmth of the hand and will then be less inclined to struggle. Speed is not advisable; take your time when catching a rat, so as not to frighten it unnecessarily. Let it be aware of your hand, even allowing it to sniff close by. This is important since rats, as essentially burrowing animals, tend to have poor eyesight.

If the rat is not used to being handled, restrain it at the base of the tail with one hand and use the other hand to hold its back, ensuring that the thumb and a finger are pressing its elbows towards the head. In this position, the rat will not be able to turn and bite you. Any pressure on the throat, however, will serve to agitate the rat, while gripping anywhere but the base of the tail will lead to injury, and may enable the rat to turn, using its tail and then its teeth to escape your grip.

Rats are highly intelligent animals, as has been borne out by laboratory

Above: *Wild Black Rat. Whether this species had any involvement in the breeding of fancy rats is unclear. Colour forms were certainly known.*

studies, and they soon adapt to being handled, showing no resentment and becoming very tame. As with all rodents, try to obtain young or newly weaned stock, because of their relatively short lifespans. This also applies to rats, particularly because young animals should ultimately prove more adaptable than older stock in a new environment. (The vital points of rats are summarized on page 112.)

Accommodation and care

Fancy rats will do well in similar quarters to those recommended for mice, bearing in mind the larger size of these animals. They tend to burrow readily, given the opportunity. Like other rodents, keep them in a relatively quiet environment; they have very sensitive hearing and will show physical signs of stress if kept in noisy surroundings. Rats are also prone to respiratory diseases. These are liable to arise in unclean surroundings, since high levels of

ammonia in their immediate vicinity can damage the lining of the respiratory tract and lay areas open to attack by a range of harmful microorganisms. To avoid such problems, always keep their quarters clean.

Very detailed studies carried out on the nutritional requirements of rats have led to the development of commercial dry pelleted rations that contain all the necessary ingredients to keep these rodents in top condition. Use this if it is available. Alternatively, feed a mixed diet based on seeds as outlined on page 24 and supplement this with fresh foods. Ensure that water is available, ideally in a drinking bottle. Rats may consume as much as 30gm (1oz) of food and 60ml (2fl.oz) of water daily, if fed on a dry pelleted diet. If you buy a large quantity of pellets, however, do keep them dry so that they do not deteriorate, and use them before the expiry date printed on the packaging. This is especially important to gain the full benefit of the vitamins, which gradually lose their potency over a period of time.

A very dry atmosphere can prove harmful both to rats and mice. Therefore, maintain a relative humidity in excess of fifty percent, otherwise signs of ringtail may become apparent. Ringtail causes the tail to become narrowed and then swell, typically towards the

Above: Rats are likely to prove prolific breeders. This Berkshire rat has a litter of twelve pups, shown here at about a week old. They are already showing their markings.

Above right: Handling a rat. Always allow a rat to be aware of your presence before attempting to handle it. They are docile creatures, and do not resent handling.

Right: An Albino rat sniffs the air. All rats tend to have poor eyesight, since they live underground and emerge after dark. The sense of smell is more significant; their whiskers are also sensory.

base. If environmental conditions are not improved, the tail may be lost. Increasing the humidity in the living quarters should resolve the condition spontaneously, however.

Breeding rats
Young male rat pups are easy to sex, even before maturity, by the relatively long ano-genital distance. (See the illustrations on page 15.) The testes should have descended into the scrotum by about three weeks of age. Hold the buck (male) in a vertical position, with its head uppermost, to be sure of spotting the testes if you are in any doubt. The rat can withdraw them back into the body. Nipples are visible in does (females) about one week after birth.

It is usual practice to separate rats into single sex groups by the time they are seven weeks old; after this time they will be approaching sexual maturity. Does are not usually used for breeding purposes until they are about thirteen weeks old and over 200gm (7oz) in weight. By comparison, males of a similar age under 275gm (9.7oz) are not usually recommended for stud purposes.

Various mating systems can be used; one particular method is to place one or two males with up to six females. This will serve to stimulate oestrus in the does as they respond to the male odours, or pheromones. Female rats cycle about every five days, so that successful matings are likely to take place soon after the introduction of a buck. The level of lighting appears important for successful breeding, since their natural prolificacy declines during the darker days of a temperate winter. Ideally, provide sufficient artificial light to give a total daily exposure of about fifteen hours. The normal gestation period is

Above: **Silver Fawn Rat**
This is a red-eyed variety, the dilute counterpart of the Agouti. The silver appearance stems from the colour of the longer guard hairs.

Below: **Agouti Rat**
The domesticated Agouti form shows more prominent brown coloration than its wild counterpart.

three weeks or so, but will be longer if mating has taken place almost immediately after the doe has given birth. She will be ready to mate again in this so-called 'post-partum' breeding period within two days of producing pups, but the developing embryos will not implant into her uterine wall as rapidly as normal. It is often best to remove the doe to

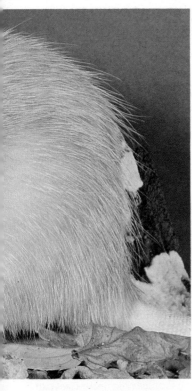

separate quarters to give birth, especially if she normally forms part of a colony. Two does may be housed together quite successfully in this way.

A litter may consist of up to fourteen pups or so. These will be independent about three weeks after birth, each young rat weighing about 50gm (1.8oz) at this stage. The doe will be ready to mate again within a week of weaning being completed, if she did not conceive at the 'post-partum' heat. Rats can breed almost until the end of their lives, but their reproductive capability declines after a year or so. Rats generally live between two and four years under normal captive circumstances, but older individuals are not uncommon.

Colour forms
Compared with mice, there are relatively few colour forms of the Fancy Rat. They can be divided into two groups: the basic colours and the recognized pattern markings.

Basic colours
White rats are certainly among the most popular varieties with the petseeker, possibly because they appear clean! There is a Pink-eyed White, which is also known as the Albino. Young rats of this variety

Below: **Cinnamon Pearl Rat**
Characterized by its dark eyes and the silvery area on its underparts. The guard hairs are chocolate.

tend to become creamy in colour as they get older. There is also a distinct Self Cream strain.

Most of the colours developed in mice are also seen in rats. The Agouti most closely resembles the ancestral Brown Rat, but the depth of brown coloration has been increased, becoming richer overall. A Silver counterpart, known as the Silver Fawn, has silver guard hairs set against a rich orange fur. The pink-eyed mutation here again exerts a diluting effect on overall

Above: **Pearl Rat**
A relatively recent innovation that corresponds to the Pearl Mouse. The hair tips are blackish or grey.

Below right: **Black Rat**
Potentially a striking variety, the depth of coloration in the Black can be poor or spoilt by odd white hairs.

Below: **Mink Rat**
A colour unique to the Rat Fancy, this black-eyed variety should be an even light coffee with a blue sheen.

Above: **Champagne Rat**
The eyes are pink and the overall coloration should be an even warm beige. White hairs are a fault.

body coloration. The Cinnamon mutation has an intermediate effect, creating a russet-brown shade of coat colour with longer chocolate guard hairs.

Among the darker colours, Self Blacks (ideally as deep as possible) and Self Chocolate (showing no trace of white) have been developed. Other varieties corresponding to the colours seen in mice are the Champagne and the Pearl, the latter being one of the more recent innovations. A colour unique to rats is the Self Mink. Ideally, these rats are coffee-

coloured, with a bluish sheen and black eyes. They are, in effect, a dilute form of the Self Chocolate.

Patterned rats
Undoubtedly the most widely seen of the patterned varieties is the Hooded Rat. The so-called hood extends from the top of the head to the face and down to the shoulders and chin. Another coloured area, the saddle, extends down the back and on to the tail. While any colour is acceptable to form the hood and saddle, the remainder of the body should be white. It is not easy to produce a top exhibition specimen of this variety. A more straightforward version is the Capped, which simply lacks the saddle but retains the coloured head. Another similar variety is the Variegated, which differs from the Capped in having a mixed rather than a white body colour, although the belly itself must remain white.

A white belly is also characteristic of the Berkshire, which should also show white feet and a similar spot on the forehead. The remainder of the body is coloured. Irish rats, by comparison, are more highly coloured, with a white area forming a small equilateral triangle on the chest. White is otherwise restricted to the feet.

Other colours
New varieties of Fancy Rat are being developed. There is a Rex form, with a curly coat and whiskers. Some interesting varieties have originated

101

Above: **Variegated Rat**
Darker colours create the best effect by emphasizing the markings. There should be a white forehead blaze and a white belly.

Below: **Berkshire Rat**
Named after the English county, the Berkshire should have symmetrical markings. A small white spot should be visible on the forehead.

Below: **Mink and Black Capped**
In this variety, the head is coloured and there is a white blaze. Capped rats of other colours can be bred.

Right: **Rex Rat**
The Rex mutation can be combined with any colour. Curly whiskers are associated with the distinctive coat.

in France, notably the Himalayan form, which was first seen around 1972. The points are darker than the body coloration, creating an attractive contrast. It does not differ significantly from the identical mutations seen in other animals, including mice and rabbits. The Himalayan itself is predominantly white in colour, whereas in the Siamese the fur is pale brown. The pairing of Himalayans together

Above: **Hooded Rat**
Also known as the English Hooded, this is the most common of the patterned varieties of fancy rat. The coloured saddle area runs down the back to the tail. The hood itself extends back to the shoulders.

should yield on average two Himalayans for every one Siamese and one Albino. Thus, a quarter of the litters should be Siamese.

Chinchillas

Whereas the preceding rodents belong to the mouse-like rodents classified in the suborder Myomorpha, chinchillas are more closely related to the guinea pig, forming one of the eighteen families in the suborder Caviomorpha.

What are chinchillas?

In the family Chinchillidae there are four species of Viscacha and two species of Chinchilla: *C.lanigeria* and *C.brevicaudata*, plus a number of subspecies. (Some experts suggest three species based on country of origin: Peruvian, *C.chinchilla*; Bolivian, *C.boliviana*; and Chilean, *C.villidera*.) Chinchillas are found at relatively high altitudes in the Andes, and had long been valued by the native Incas for their fur. Subsequently, this also became very popular in Europe during the eighteenth and nineteenth centuries, to the extent that there was considerable concern as to whether the chinchilla populations would survive such persecution.

The fur of the Chinchilla also accounts largely for its appeal as a pet. Each individual hair follicle can bear up to eighty hairs, which produces a very dense coat that provides protection against the cold and effectively excludes parasites. Longer guard hairs are also apparent in the coat.

Chinchillas use their long, powerful hind limbs to provide much of the thrust for movement, progressing largely by hopping or jumping in the same way as rabbits. Like rats, chinchillas will use the paws to hold food and tend to become more active towards dusk. They become tame and friendly, but are not too keen on being handled.

The first attempts at setting up captive breeding colonies took place in South America, and then in 1923 M.F. Chapman, a mining engineer, returned to the United States with a breeding nucleus of eight male and three female chinchillas. They proved adaptable creatures, being unaffected by the difference in altitude or the other changes that they encountered. Today, commercial breeding units offering chinchillas are quite widespread, although their care tends to be more specialized than for the other rodents featured in this guide and they are therefore correspondingly expensive.

Handling

Always handle chinchillas carefully to avoid damaging the coat. It is

Below: *Pink White Chinchilla feeding. Although pelleted diets are normally used for these animals, also offer good quality hay.*

Above: *Dust baths are very important for chinchillas, serving to keep their unique coats in top condition. Use only the correct dust material, normally changed daily.*

Below: *A breeding cage, shown outside on grass for convenience only. The wire 'tunnel' allows the male to enter each of the cages; each female wears a collar to prevent it leaving the 'compartment'.*

best to restrain them by holding the base of the tail with one hand and the rest of the body with the other hand. Although they are usually docile, chinchillas do have sharp teeth and you must bear this in mind when handling them.

Accommodation and care
Chinchillas need a dry environment and cannot be kept satisfactorily out-of-doors, like guinea pigs. The

usual way of accommodating them is in an enclosure with a wire-mesh floor, so that droppings and urine fall beneath, where they will not contaminate the chinchilla's fur. A nestbox can be provided, ideally about 25cm (10in) in height and width and 50cm (20in) in length. Make this solidly from wood and fix it in such a way that you can close the chinchilla within, if required, when cleaning out the cage for example. Also make sure you can inspect the inside of the box easily.

A vital piece of equipment that you must provide for chinchillas is a dust bath, which they will use to keep their coat in top condition. Use a shallow container with sides about 12.5cm (5in) high. In some designs the sides continue over to form a roof – rather like a cylinder open at both ends. Use a metal bath or one that the chinchilla will not be able to destroy with its teeth. Put this into the cage for a short period each day, and change the contents regularly. The 'dust' material is either volcanic ash or activated clay and is easily obtainable from your supplier under a number of commercial names.

Above: *A Standard Chinchilla in a natural-looking setting. These South American rodents from the Andes Mountains were first kept in captivity for their dense fur.*

Below: *Chinchillas may use a nestbox for sleeping. Ensure that it is kept clean; you may provide straw bedding, but it is not strictly needed.*

The diet of chinchillas is usually based on specially formulated pellets, typically augmented with hay. This is essential for providing roughage in the diet. Ensure that it is of top quality, such as clover hay, and store it in a dry locality, along with the pellets. Never use mouldy or dusty hay, since it is potentially dangerous. Providing fresh greenfood and root vegetables, such as carrot, may also be beneficial. Offer only small amounts to minimize the risk of scouring. (See also page 29.)

Breeding chinchillas

It is usual to pair chinchillas up when they are about six months old. The ano-genital gap again provides the means of sexing these rodents, being shorter in the female. Fighting between members of a pair is uncommon, although mating also is rarely observed. The most obvious sign of breeding activity is likely to be the presence of a so-called 'stopper', which is whitish in colour and expelled by the female following mating. The stopper rapidly shrivels outside the body and is easy to miss as a result. It may not be apparent in

Below: *A Brown Velvet female with a Standard youngster. Chinchillas will breed readily, usually producing two offspring – known as kits. Gestation can be up to 128 days.*

all instances, however, but can be a useful guide.

When in breeding condition, the male may coo and rub his chin around the nesting box, a gesture sometimes reciprocated by the female. If she appears aggressive, however, it may be best to separate them and then re-introduce them on neutral territory. This is certainly recommended when pairing adult stock. In fact, there are various mating systems, and often commercial breeders may run one male with several females via a series of interconnecting cages.

The gestation period is variable within the range 111-128 days, and this may depend on the species. One of the first clear external signs of pregnancy will be the enlargement and reddening of the female's mammary glands after about sixty days. Avoid handling her for examination from this point onwards. As the impending birth approaches, add milk powder to the female's diet and check that any nestbox is clean. In addition, the floor of the cage should be lined with paper towelling to prevent injury and assist drying of the young at birth. Withdraw the dust bath several days before the expected birth, as this could irritate her genital organs at this stage, and wait until a week after the birth before re-introducing it.

Litters tend to be small in number.

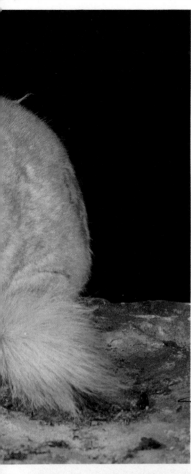

compared with other rodents. The average is about two kits (as young chinchillas are known) per litter, but as many as eight have been born on rare occasions. The female will undergo a post-partum oestrus following their birth, and may mate with a male at this time.

After the relatively long gestation period, kits are born in an advanced state of development, complete with a covering of fur. They are also able to move, but are also extremely wet and could succumb in cold conditions. It is sensible to keep a watch on their development, as this can also indicate a problem with the female, such as a local infection of a mammary gland. Difficulties are more likely with larger litters.

It is normal for the female to loose the fur around her nipples as the kits suckle, but this will ultimately

Left: **Beige Chinchilla**
This form was first bred in 1960 in the USA. The original example was weak, but survived with care.

Below left: **Silver Chinchilla**
This is one of the White forms. Others include the Mosaic. Colours are as easy to keep as the Standard.

Below: **Black Velvet Chinchilla**
One of the darker varieties, the Black form originally appeared in the United States during 1960.

Above: **Pink White Chinchilla**
*This attractive colour form, also
known as Starlight, is one of three
white mutations of the Chinchilla.*

Right: **Standard x Charcoal**
*This is lighter in colour than the pure
Charcoal. New colours are being
developed; one of the more recent is
a violet form from Zimbabwe.*

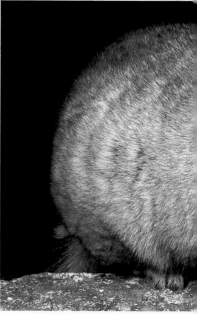

regrow. Sharp teeth may cause the
dam to reject the attentions of her
offspring when they attempt to
suckle. These will need to be filed
down carefully when apparent. If a
foster-parent is required, with a
large litter for example, then a
suckling guinea pig provides a
realistic alternative to hand-rearing
and will usually accept chinchilla
offspring without problems.
    A human infant food based on
cereal products can be especially
useful for chinchillas before
weaning. This usually takes place

Above: **Brown Velvet Chinchilla**
The name of this mutation reflects not only the basic coat colour but also the superb softness of the fur.

after seven weeks or so. In any event, be sure to separate young chinchillas by the time they are four months old.

Breeding stock is considered to be at its peak at four years of age. The lifespan of chinchillas can be up to twenty years, making them the longest lived rodents featured.

Colour forms
The natural coloration of chinchillas is a slate blue-grey with a white belly

fur, known as the Standard variety. Many colour mutations are available, including White (with varieties Mosaic, Silver, and Starlight/Pink White), Beige, Black Velvet, Brown Velvet, Charcoal, Ebony, Pastels and a variety of crosses, although these may be relatively expensive. Some mutations take many years to develop and there is the potential for many more as breeding techniques advance.

The exhibition side of chinchilla keeping is rapidly expanding around the world, with a growing number of shows, many combined with other small mammal exhibitions.

Summary table

	GERBIL	HAMSTER
Adult weight	(F) 75gm 2.6oz (M) 85gm 3.0oz	(F) 120gm 4.2oz (M) 108gm 3.8oz
Life span	4-5 yrs	2-2.5 yrs
Body temperature	36.4-37.9°C 97.5-100.2°F	36.2-37.5°C 97.2-99.5°F
Duration of mating period	12-18 hours	4-24 hours
Gap between mating periods	4 days	4 days
Normal length of gestation	24-25 days	16-18 days
Normal litter size	5	6-8
Eyes open at	10-12 days	15 days
Nursing period	21-24 days	20-24 days
Eating solid food at	17-18 days	7-9 days
Breeding life	15-20 mths	11-18 mths

MOUSE	RAT	CHINCHILLA
(F) 30gm 1.1oz (M) 30gm 1.1oz	(F) 300gm 10.5oz (M) 500gm 17.6oz	(F) 595gm 21oz (M) 510gm 18oz
1-2 yrs	2-4 yrs	Up to 20 yrs
35.7-37.7°C 96.4-100°F	37.5-38.2°C 99.5-100.8°F	36.9-37.7°C 98.4-100°F
9-20 hours	9-20 hours	4 days
5 days	5 days	28-35 days
19-21 days	21-23 days	111-128 days
9-12	9-11	2-4
12-13 days	10-12 days	At birth
16-21 days	21 days	42 days
12-13 days	10-12 days	12-14 days
12-18 mths	14+ mths	7-96 mths

Index to species

Page numbers in **bold** indicate major references, including accompanying photographs. Page numbers in *italics* indicate other illustrations. Less important text entries are shown in normal type.

Further reading

Cooke, A. *Exhibition and Pet Mice* Saiga Publishing, 1977

Denham, K. *Guinea Pigs and Chinchillas* Bartholomew, 1977

Hanney, P. *Rodents – Their Lives and Habits* David and Charles, 1975

Henwood, C. *Love Your Gerbil* Foulsham, 1985

Henwood, C. *Love Your Hamster* Foulsham, 1984

Jones, A. *Encyclopedia of Pet Mice* TFH Publications, 1979

MacDonald, D. (ed) *The Encyclopedia of Mammals* George Allen and Unwin, 1984

Robinson, D. *The Right Way to Keep Hamsters* Elliot Right Way Books 1977

Robinson, D. *Exhibition and Pet Hamsters and Gerbils* Saiga Publishing, 1979

Robinson, D. *Encyclopedia of Gerbils* TFH Publications, 1980

Smith, K.W. *Hamsters and Gerbils* Bartholomew, 1976

Smith, K.W. *Mice and Rats* Bartholomew, 1976

Snow, C.F. *Chinchilla Breeding* Foyles, 1959

Picture credits

Artists
Copyright of the artwork illustrations on the pages following the artists' names is the property of Salamander Books Ltd.

Graeme Campbell Design: 36-7, 38-9, 63

Clifford and Wendy Meadway: 16, 19, 22-3,

Guy Troughton: 12, 13, 15, 24, 36-7, 38-9

Photographs
The publishers wish to thank the following photographers and agencies who have supplied photographs for this book. The photographs have been credited by page number and position on the page: (B)Bottom, (T)Top, (C)Centre, (BL)Bottom left etc.

Heather Angel/Biofotos: 48-9(T)

Ardea London: 15, 26, 44(I.Beames), 62(I.Beames), 79, 80(B)

Michael Chinery: 13

Marc Henrie: Half-title page, 18, 46, 49(B), 52-3(B), 54, 56(B), 57(B), 64, 66, 67, 68, 69, 70, 71, 72(B), 73(B), 74, 75, 76(B), 77

David Hosking: 42, 50-1, 56-7(T), 95

Ideas into Print: 10-11, 14, 17, 20, 25, 61

Cyril Laubscher: Title page, Copyright page, 40-1, 43, 47, 52-3(T), 54-5, 58, 59, 60, 72(T), 73(T), 76(T), 78(B), 80(T), 81, 82, 83, 84, 85, 86, 87, 88, 89, 90, 91, 92, 93, 96, 97, 98, 99, 100, 101(B), 102, 103, 104, 105(T), 106, 107, 108, 109, 110, 111

Press-tige Pictures Ltd: Endpapers, 27, 65, 94, 101(T), 105(B)

Peter W. Scott: 30, 32(TR), 33

Royal Veterinary College, Laboratory Animal Science Unit: 29, 31, 32(TL)

Acknowledgements
The publishers wish to thank the following for their help in preparing this book: Animal Crackers Petshop, Animal Magic Petshop, John Burnett (Sonnett Ranch Chinchillas), Paul Chaplin, Irene Christie, Mike Davis, Tony Holland, Eric Jukes, Deborah Kenyon, Craig and Ryan Laubscher, Stanley Maughan, Mick Plose, Pat and Rosemary Quaid, Simon Rivett, Stuart Smith, John Strutt, and White's Pet Centre. Karen Ramsay (for editorial assistance), Rita Hemsley (for typing the author's manuscript).

The illustration on page 63 is based on a concept on page 19 of 'Hamsters and Gerbils', Bartholomew Pet Care Series.

Companion volumes of interest:

A PETKEEPER'S GUIDE TO REPTILES AND AMPHIBIANS
A FISHKEEPER'S GUIDE TO THE TROPICAL AQUARIUM
A FISHKEEPER'S GUIDE TO COMMUNITY FISHES
A FISHKEEPER'S GUIDE TO COLDWATER FISHES
A FISHKEEPER'S GUIDE TO MARINE FISHES
A FISHKEEPER'S GUIDE TO MAINTAINING A HEALTHY AQUARIUM
A FISHKEEPER'S GUIDE TO GARDEN PONDS
A FISHKEEPER'S GUIDE TO AQUARIUM PLANTS
A FISHKEEPER'S GUIDE TO CENTRAL AMERICAN CICHLIDS
A FISHKEEPER'S GUIDE TO FISH BREEDING
A FISHKEEPER'S GUIDE TO AFRICAN AND ASIAN CATFISHES